D1286925

CREATIVE ASTROLOGY

Prudence Jones is an astrologer of thirteen years' standing. She has worked in Creative Astrology since 1983 and has led many workshops, plus an ongoing growth group, in Cambridge and in London. She trained in humanistic psychotherapy with the Minster Centre, London, and practises as a therapist and astrologer in Cambridge. Since 1984 she has been a focal organiser of the Glastonbury (now Oak Dragon) Living Astrology Camps, and is a regular speaker at Astrological Association meetings. Her interest in ancient astronomy and calendars has led to a series of lectures, pamphlets and articles presenting original research. She is a key organiser in the Pagan Federation (the coordinating body for European Paganism), and has contributed substantially to contemporary understanding of the symbol of the Holy Grail.

CREATIVE ASTROLOGY

Experiential Understanding of the Birth Chart

Edited by
PRUDENCE JONES

The Aquarian Press
An Imprint of HarperCollins*Publishers*

The Aquarian Press
An Imprint of GraftonBooks
A Division of HarperCollins*Publishers*
77–85 Fulham Palace Road,
Hammersmith, London W6 8JB

Published by the The Aquarian Press 1991
1   3   5   7   9   10   8   6   4   2

© Prudence Jones 1991

Prudence Jones asserts the moral right to
be identified as the author of this work

A CIP catalogue record for this book
is available from the British Library

ISBN 1–85538–110–9

Typeset by Selectmove Ltd, London
Printed in Great Britain by
Biddles Limited, Guildford, Surrey

All rights reserved. No part of this publication may be
reproduced, stored in a retrieval system, or transmitted,
in any form or by any means, electronic, mechanical
photocopying, recording or otherwise, without the prior
permission of the publishers.

Contents

To Sunna,
who inspires our creativity,

and to Saturn,
who challenges and sustains it

Acknowledgements

Several people, unnamed in these pages, helped lay the groundwork for this book.

Alix Pirani and Jane Malcolmson, who in the early 1980s ran a series of workshops on Creative Mythology, gave me the paradigm for what I later called Creative Astrology. This format showed me how to bring the archetypes alive. Later, Gabrielle Oliver, whose proposed arts and human potential centre, Creative Space, was an idea before its time, helped conceptualise the link between creativity, inspiration and insight.

In what follows, the quotation from Roberto Assagioli is reprinted by kind permission of Messrs HarperCollins, that from Marion Sutherland by Messrs Longman Ltd, and that from Carl Rogers by Charles E. Merrill Publishing International. The quotation from Cherry Gilchrist is reproduced by permission of the author and the Astrological Association of Great Britain, and that from Maritha Pottenger by permission of T.I.A. Publications, Los Angeles. Nigel Pennick provided the draughtsmanship for Figures 7 and 10, and the whole volume was kept on course by Marion Russell, a most patient and perceptive editor.

Introduction

This book presents the insights of twelve people who have pioneered the reintroduction of practical symbolism into astrology. Creative, experiential, or 'living' astrology is an approach which was developed independently by many practitioners during the 1980s, on both sides of the Atlantic. All of the contributors to this book were pioneers in the field, and they have all brought their unique outlook and insights to bear on its development. The personal histories, theoretical arguments, musings, case studies and specific exercises which this book contains illustrate considerable differences of emphasis and approach. What emerges from these, nevertheless, proves to be a set of variations on a common theme. That theme is a determination to expose the tacit knowledge which shapes the day-to-day experience of us all.

A New Map of the Mind

Astrology has traditionally been seen as a descriptive process, communicating information from an expert to an enquirer, from the astrologer to the client. To most outsiders, astrology is concerned with predicting the future, and the astrologer is judged by his or her accuracy in achieving this result. Astrologers are popularly supposed to tell their clients what is likely to happen, and perhaps advise on what the client should do about it. Such an approach may be appropriate in fields such as mundane astrology (reading, interpreting and anticipating socio-political developments), financial astrology, especially dealing with Stock Market trends, and of course horary astrology – the use of astrology to answer specific questions such as 'Where is my lost dog?' In these fields the astrologer is concerned primarily with knowledge of the outside world, knowledge which can be imparted factually from expert to enquirer, for the enquirer to use as he or she pleases. During this century, by contrast, astrology in the West has become increasingly concerned with the inner world, with psychology. Character delineation, the interpretation of the individual natal chart, has become central to the astrologer's practice, and for modern psychological astrologers, character is destiny.

Why should this be? Analysis of the inner or visionary world has usually been part of the 'underground tradition', esoteric philosophy or the secret teachings of mystics from most systems of religious thought. This sees the 'outer' world and the 'inner' world as reflections of each other, in essence identical despite their apparent divergence. Some spiritual travellers are gifted with the intuition or vision of this hidden unity; others simply take it as a working hypothesis. A change in the 'inner', spiritual world of attitudes, aims and values is said by the hidden tradition to coincide mysteriously (magically) with an otherwise inexplicable change in the 'outer', material world of other people and objects. It is this tradition to which modern psychological astrology is heir.

Modern astrology has its roots in Theosophical thought which in the late nineteenth century introduced Hindu and Buddhist cosmology to the West. The astrologer Alan Leo (W. H. Allen, 1860–1917) joined the Theosophical Society in 1890, and after marrying another Theosophist, Bessie Phillips, changed the slant of his vastly successful practice from traditional astrology, concerned with the prediction and analysis of the outer events, to the astrological analysis of the psyche, the 'inner man' of esoteric teaching, which is said to guide both the character and the 'fate' of the outer person. This idea of the 'inner man', the greater or higher or deeper Self, towards which the lesser self can grow in wisdom and responsibility, is a commonplace nowadays in

2

New Age circles. For modern psychological astrologers, the natal horoscope describes or at least indicates the nature of this greater Self, whereas for most earlier astrologers, the natal horoscope was simply a description of the individual's life circumstances, neither willed nor meaningful, but simply fated.

Thus, as almost all readers of this volume will know, the modern psychological astrologer reads character, our subjective reality, rather than destiny, our objective circumstances, from the information on the natal horoscope. The natal horoscope is said to describe what a person will experience rather than the external agencies – the 'objective' facts – which are seen as merely bringing about such experiences. During the twentieth century, astrological practice has dealt with methods of psychological interpretation in preference to methods of predicting material circumstances. A characteristic pattern of feeling oppressed by authority-figures, for example, does not of itself imply that one's father was cruel, or that one's employer will be unjust, although either or both of these situations might express the pattern. Material circumstances are simply possible expressions of the inner psychological blueprint.

Nevertheless, the extent to which the inner person guides outer circumstances is not something which mainstream Western psychology has been able to accommodate. The psychology of modern astrologers is not that of the commonsensical Western materialist. For the last 300 years or so, Western 'common sense' has believed that people are independent agents, the masters, colleagues or victims of others in an outside world which is intrinsically independent of them. Hence, Western psychology has aimed at a model of ego-strength and self-reliance, tempered with such affiliative needs or social skills as are thought necessary for social cohesion. Unitive experiences of a visionary sort, even those involving more low-key hunches or telepathy, have been taken as pathological or at the very least marginalised as anomalous.

3

Curiously enough, at the same time that Theosophy and other esoteric movements entered popular consciousness in the 1890s, the rational consensus reality was also being challenged by a medical theory of 'occult', hidden causes. This was psychoanalysis, a secular system which asserted the existence of an unrecognised, unconscious Self whose motives helped determine the actions of the conscious ego. The cure of psychological disorders such as phobias, obsessions and fugues did not consist according to this system in a rational procedure such as retraining the sufferer's actions (behaviour therapy), or retraining their thoughts and feelings (hypnotherapy). It consisted in the non-rational procedure of recognising, acknowledging and coming to terms with the vast world of the unconscious. By experiencing and accepting emotions, memories or thoughts which had previously been hidden, so Freud and his followers discovered, the sufferer spontaneously perceives the problem in a different and somehow less intractable form. The way in which problems become manageable through this method remains a mystery to the rational, concrete mind.

Psychoanalysis developed, and remains workable, as a purely materialistic system, the undoing of psychological traumas suffered and forgotten in the early life of a given individual. Nevertheless, the idea of the unconscious Self which it introduced into secular Western thought has far-reaching implications for our hard-won 'commonsensical' view of ethical and legal responsibility. To what extent are people truly responsible for their actions? The effects of Freud's terminology for our legal and social institutions have yet to be worked through. Its effects on the philosophy of mind have as yet been negligible.

Some of Freud's successors in analytical psychotherapy, most notably Dr Carl Jung, who introduced the ideas of wholeness, synchronicity, individuation and the active imagination (q.v.) into analytical technique, and Dr Roberto Assagioli, with his more actively creative school of Psychosynthesis, supplemented analytical understanding of the origin of psychological dysfunction in early trauma with a more philosophical, conceptual concern for enabling each patient to assign a sense of meaning to their own life. Among these innovators the work of the analyst extended beyond that of a physician of the mind, towards that of a spiritual director in the religious sense. Analysts began to face the reality of the inner person behind the outer character and its adaptations to the world, and to tackle the question about how this inner, greater, or deeper Self actually affects the life of its owner. Psychological theory was catching up with esoteric tradition.

The implications for astrologers were simply that esoteric astrology, originally couched in the spiritual terminology of Theosophy, could now use a secular vocabulary. The natal horoscope could now be read as a pattern of character, of the talents, liabilities and reaction patterns which define each individual personality and which go beyond the personality as it is already known to its owner. The horoscope defines likely experiences rather than fated events, and the people and situations in a person's life are understood to be significant primarily as expressions of the enquirer's own psychological landscape. Although many if not most enquirers still come to the astrologer expecting predictions about the outside world, psychological terminology makes sense and is satisfying to most people, and so the new inwardly oriented astrology has become the norm in Western practice. It has several advantages. It puts people at the centre of their own universe, allowing them to interpret the world from their own perspective rather than according to the norms of people around them, norms which have usually proved unsatisfactory by the time they think of contacting an astrologer. Furthermore, the events of a person's life start to seem significant rather than random. A life-plan emerges, and the future begins to be sensed and planned for, as a natural outgrowth of one's inner blueprint rather than as something either willed by arbitrary choice, or imposed upon one by early trauma or by hostile Fate.

A New Method of Interpretation

Nevertheless, clients still come to the astrologer asking for help with very specific personal dilemmas. Since astrologers can no longer tell from the natal chart whether the client's spouse will leave them, whether they will lose their job, develop terminal cancer or any other of a myriad other possibilities bravely faced, the expert is forced to introduce the enquirer to the more abstract version of causality and prediction with which modern astrology deals. This is often done by direct experience, generally using methods drawn from secular psychotherapy. By focusing on the psychological patterns described in the horoscope as well as on unacknowledged themes in the client's own presentation, the astrologer subtly guides the enquirer towards experiencing and owning those attitudes of character of which they had previously been unaware. In this way, as in ordinary psychotherapy, the problem with which the client presented the counsellor may be mysteriously resolved. Astrology provides a map of the client's intrinsic nature, and ordinary psychodynamics show what aspect of that wholeness or potential is uppermost in the client's experience at the time of the session. Armed with these two sets of information, the counselling astrologer goes to work.

This method, however, still leaves a great deal of power in the hands of the practitioner, who can reasonably be seen as subtly manipulating the enquirer according to a hidden schedule known only to him- or herself. The client or enquirer is still dependent on an outside expert to reveal arcane hidden truths. There is nothing intrinsically wrong with such an imbalance of power, indeed sometimes a mysteriously all-knowing expert is exactly what we need. But astrological interpretation is not of itself obscure: if astrology is universally true, then there is some part of us that is in tune with it at all times. The challenge lies in gaining access to that part. We are left facing the earlier question: how is it that the inner person of esoteric theory actually influences the outer person and their life circumstances?

Creative Astrology approaches this challenge directly. It gives the power of interpretation back to the client. By carrying out exercises in practical symbolism, exercises such as guided fantasy, role-playing, the use of painting, sound, dance and body language, the enquirer can contact their own unconscious assumptions, enlarge their sphere of personal awareness, and, most importantly, through the very act of exploring this symbolic hinterland, begin to reshape the whole structure of their psyche, known and unknown, in a more personally satisfying way. The creative approach not only imparts a sense of significance to the events of a person's life, but it also gives the recipient the means of keeping that understanding alive.

It does this by awakening the recipient's power of interpretation. Earlier approaches to psychology, to spirituality, and of course to astrology, had assumed that the ability to interpret was only gained after years of study. To be sure, both skill and experience need talent and effort to develop. But since astrologers must assume that some part of every person is in tune with astrological cycles, then an intuitive ability to interpret its signals for oneself would seem to lie dormant in us all. Creative Astrology simply gives us access to that ability.

Creative Astrology seems to have come into being towards the end of the 1970s. Many of its techniques and much of its philosophy come from the psychological revolution of the 1960s and 1970s, in particular from the Human Potential Movement. Several of the essays in this collection describe their authors' own emergence from this movement. The Human Potential Movement, calling itself the 'third force in psychology' after psychoanalysis and behaviourism, was developed in the 1930s and 1940s, reaching a peak of high profile in the 1960s and 1970s. Humanistic psychologists saw themselves as concerned not simply with understanding and undoing early trauma, as mainstream psychoanalysts were,

7

nor yet only with skills training and behaviour modification, as was the behaviouristic school, but with unlocking the hidden potential of every person, whether sick or well. Workshops using fantasy, drama, dance, the use of painting, body language and sound tapped the spontaneity of the unconscious mind and allowed people to contact attitudes, habits, prejudices and also resources of character which they had never dreamed they possessed. Humanistic psychology has been from the start a tool for growth as well as for healing.

Unlike transpersonal analysts of the post-Freudian school, the early humanistic psychologists were concerned to share the power of interpretation with their clients, empowering the latter at an early stage to enter into dialogue with their own unconscious. In this emphasis on means and methods, demystifying the process of becoming whole rather than leaving it in the hands of an all-knowing analyst, many humanistic psychologists developed a strong emphasis on encouraging personal responsibility, rather than what was seen as the 'victim mentality' of the identified patient. The victim's ploy of blaming society or their upbringing (or indeed their stars) for what was wrong with their life was perceived as inadequate. What became important was not what had been done to a person, but how they themselves had adapted to it and persisted in living out their adaptation, despite opportunities to step into a more satisfying role. How and to what extent did people create their own reality? The exploratory techniques developed in the Human Potential Movement for contacting the spontaneous, non-rational part of each person were used to test out such questions. They were easily adapted by practitioners of the anti-fatalistic, experiential approach which became Creative Astrology.

One early writer on creative techniques, Maritha Pottenger in *Encounter Astrology* (1978), is quite clear about her debt to this movement. 'This book is an addition to the toolkits of those of us active in the spiral of growth and self-actualization,' she states. 'My emphasis is on self-actualization . . . the tool [i.e. astrology] is secondary.' Here astrology is seen simply as an aid to psychology. The twelve signs of the zodiac are a mandala of wholeness, one of several psychological models of health, and every individual should become skilled in living each of them. Here there is no concession to the inbuilt bias of the personal birth chart: wholeness is all, and the psyche is potentially infinite.

In the UK, by contrast, the early development of this approach seems to have come from esoteric theory, the roots of the original psychological astrology of the 1890s. Beginning in 1978, Cherry Gilchrist ran Creative Astrology workshops, so-called partly in reference to the esoteric tradition of Cabbala (see Glossary). She later set up the Orbis School of Creative Astrology, which ran for several years in the early 1980s. Here the aim was once more not to interpret people's horoscopes, but to use practical and contemplative exercises to help students grasp the nature of the ten planetary principles for themselves. Here creative techniques were an aid to the better understanding of astrology, which itself extends far beyond the field of personal psychology.

Cabbalistic tradition recognises four levels, or 'worlds', of reality, of which the second most abstract, nearer to us than the ineffable Absolute, is known as the Creative World, the universe of thought. This is the realm from which inspiration comes. It is creative for two reasons: it expresses the creative outpouring of the Absolute, and it also sparks off the creative activities of human beings, who endeavour to convey its insights by means of words and images. For example, the essence of aggression or assertiveness, itself an abstract concept, can be symbolised or represented by a soldier, or by the blade of a knife, or by the taste of chilli pepper, and so on. None of these symbols is itself the only correct one, but only a person who has adequately grasped the underlying concept or archetype which exists in the Creative World can recognise whether any of them is appropriate or not. In this way, Creative Astrology is a training of the intuition, and thus a practical esoteric discipline.

Using creative techniques for exploration of the astrological principles is a more radical procedure than using them to explore personal truths in therapy and growth. It relies entirely on our trust in the objectivity of human intuition. Although nowadays astrology is heavily biased towards observation and statistical corroboration, in practice it has always had a significant theoretical input from seers and mediums, people whose intuition alone gave them information about the field. Now, with the rediscovery of practical symbolism through Creative Astrology, the methods of the visionary and the intuitive have become open to all. To be sure, not every workshop participant is going to turn out to be a gifted seer, and workshop leaders do require some skill in distinguishing genuine insights by participants from the results of personal bias, poor concentration or misunderstanding. Nevertheless, the creative techniques used in the workshops do indeed seem to unlock the intuitive sense possessed, to however small a degree, by everyone. In this way Creative Astrology is a completely new departure in astrological teaching and exploration.

The methods of humanistic psychology itself were drawn partly from spiritual exercises. These have been largely lacking, for a variety of reasons, in Western Christianity, but certain techniques of Eastern religion in particular are disciplined methods for contacting the intuitive sense of spirituality which is said to reside in each person. They presuppose a model of human psychology which includes a transcendental component – that is, not simply the individualistic, materialistic model of Western 'common sense'. In its affirmation of practical intuitive symbolism, Creative Astrology bridges the existing gaps between astrology, psychology, spirituality and magic. Now that transpersonal psychology has become a recognised part of the modern psychological field, protected by this aura of comparative respectability, astrologers might feel free once more to return to their esoteric roots.

This Book

The essays in the present collection run the whole gamut from client-centred personal interpretation to the use of astrology in ritual magic. The shift from expert–client interpretation to creative exploration is not confined to astrology. In her contribution to this collection, Tina Whitehead describes how the techniques now used in Creative Astrology have been utilised for many years in 'pupil-centred' teaching, where the teacher no longer imparts information to a passive audience but guides the pupil in a process of personal discovery. What people discover for themselves, sticks. What is imparted by an expert, however apposite or valuable it may be, can easily be forgotten. In mainstream psychotherapy, too, the process of authoritative interpretation by the analyst has been radically supplemented by the 'person-centred' approach of Carl Rogers. The role of the expert as facilitator of the enquirer's discoveries, rather than as imparter of cast-iron facts, has quietly become established in all kinds of disciplines over the last 50–60 years.

Babs Kirby and Lindsay River each describe one specific imaginative exercise which will help bring an aspect of the horoscope to life for the person who experiments with it. The insights that can be gained from such an experiment are far more informative than even the most detailed reading of astrological textbooks on that topic could provide: they are couched in the enquirer's own language and are automatically pitched at a level that the enquirer can understand. They contain references known only to the enquirer, which an outside consultant could not possibly know were relevant. In a creative writing exercise such as Lindsay's, the pace of discovery itself is in the hands of the explorer and there is no danger of the psychological 'indigestion' which can happen when information is accessed too rapidly. As both these authors and others in the collection stress, creative methods are non-invasive and respectful of the recipient's reality. Because it is the recipient him- or herself who is creating the results, these methods are empowering. They give the recipient a sense of achievement and discovery, a sense which can percolate through into other areas of life and restore a person's sense of meaning and confidence.

The Suffolk astrologers, whose essay ends the collection, also stress how important it is in a leaderless group to take exploration at the pace dictated by the enquirer. This essay contains fascinating accounts of discoveries made in an ongoing leaderless group, even the use of creative techniques to rectify the birthtime! They also stress that an atmosphere of trust and security is essential if people are to risk exploring painful areas of experience. This is not simply trust of the other people in the group, but is the whole group's trust of the unconscious processes of the psyche itself, which will bring unacknowledged issues to the surface of consciousness when the enquirer is ready to explore them and not before. As astrologers, we have faith in the gradual development of ourselves and the rest of the cosmos, and in any case we can often anticipate the likely time of a person's discoveries by progressions and transits to their natal chart. Non-astrological growth groups, without such an individualised time-scale for personal development, are more easily tempted to break down 'resistances' to insight in what can be a traumatic way. The Suffolk astrologers are particularly insistent on the need to respect each enquirer's pace of change. The success of their group over the last seven years bears out the wisdom of this approach.

The articles by Hans Planje, Jochen and Ulrike Encke, and Palden Jenkins discuss the holistic theory behind astrological correspondences more directly. Jochen and Ulrike write from a more traditionally therapist-centred viewpoint, in which the group is guided by the therapist, pushed and supported through unpleasant experiences which lead to resolution and insight. Nevertheless, here the interconnectedness of all things, a basic tenet of astrological theory, makes itself felt. The examples given by the Enckes show how it may mysteriously turn out for example that participants in an astrological psychotherapy group just happen to be living through personal dilemmas corresponding to the planetary roles they have been allotted in the enactment of a different group member's horoscope. We see how the traditional psychotherapeutic monsters of transference and counter-transference, projection and introjection, must be redefined by the psychological astrologer as a normal, inevitable and indeed helpful aspect of human interaction as mirrored in the horoscope. We see how the distinctions between group identity and individual identity, personal psychology and outer material reality break down when the symbolism of the horoscope is brought to life through imaginative discussion and role-play.

Hans Planje, too, proposes that astrology originated at a time when the distinctions between subjective and objective, individual and collective were not so sharply drawn as they are now. The purpose of astrodrama, his preferred therapeutic technique, is likewise 'to rediscover connections . . . to fill up and complete the proliferation of individual energies with a holistic relation to the universe'. By using movement, dialogue, role-play and other activities in a deliberate enactment of a given horoscope, group participants not only discover more about that horoscope in particular, but also experience how the astrology of the moment describes the group itself and its setting, the by now familiar synchro-nicities of a representative of officialdom arriving 'by chance' during a Saturn workshop, for example, or the lights fusing during a workshop about Uranus.

This mirroring of subjective, individual issues in the collective world, the macrocosm or greater reality which according to 'commonsense' Western reality has nothing to do with the individual, is of course central to astrological theory. It has nevertheless come as a surprise to discover how Creative Astrology, originally conceived as a re-em-powerment of the individual, who can so easily feel overawed by the fatalism of planetary trends, has itself brought direct experience of our interconnectedness with the whole. Palden Jenkins, who describes his Living Astrology camps in this collection, began, however, by working deliberately with large group dynamics in order to explore the relationship between astrologers' structured knowledge of themselves and their situation, and the spontaneity which is an inescapable part of day-to-day living in a closed group. As with small groups, so with large groups: the result is often 'a series of group "miracles"', as Palden tells us. '*Everyone* seems to find what they need, plus more, and is empowered and enthused to make great further progress at home, not only in astrology but in the resolution of crucial life issues.' In these groups the aim is education, not therapy; but in some way therapy results from the experience. By creatively embodying objective or collective situations, such as the planetary positions of the day, or their local space positions as seen from the campsite, participants unwittingly discover something that is relevant and healing for their personal situation. From astrological theory, this is to be expected, but it is creative techniques that show us how to bring it about.

In his article, Palden also describes more left-brain ways of attuning people to the dance of the planets. In their concern with individual psychology or even the forecasting of events, astrologers easily forget the magnificent spectacle of the turning of the heavens, and the experience of cycles – the daily, the monthly, the seasonal cycle – which living out of doors can give. Workshops in which people simply pace out the current planetary cycles according to the ephemeris can be enlightening as well as enjoyable. Participants become aware of how the movements of the planets are constantly at work in their lives, through the calendar and the landscape, as well as simply activating their own natal horoscope.

In my own essay I discuss the role of creativity in relating the outer, objective world to the inner, subjective one, and indeed in mediating between other dualities such as fate and free will, mind and matter, secular and sacred reality. My examples are drawn from teaching and therapy, but the model which explains them best is one derived from ancient and modern ritual, the model of the sacred space between the worlds, a closed environment in which miracles may happen. Helene Hess's essay deals with ritual directly. She shows how ritual serves to attune people, consciously and unconsciously, to the turning of the seasons and of greater astrological cycles.

Helene likewise points out that standard astrological interpretation in terms of character drives and statistical patterns is less useful in a ritual context than direct contemplation of the mythological attributions of the stars and planets. In a sense the stars and planets are bringing their associated deities or spirits into the ritual, and they are best interpreted on that level. Creativity here involves theatrical activity, and also the 'coincidences' that happen after a ritual, which as Helene writes 'reflect something in a concrete form of what was being sown at the time in the collective unconscious of humanity . . . being reflected microcosmically within the ritual'. Whether or not we agree that rituals affect the world directly we can certainly accept that a ritual or dramatic performance which is timed by the rising, culmination and setting of the stars and planets can put its participants in harmony with the archetypal ideas which are manifesting at the time.

Timing a ritual or a celebration according to the planets can be done most spectacularly out of doors. As Palden Jenkins points out in his essay, one such ritual, the re-enactment of an ancient Roman celebration of the goddess Venus, was timed exactly by the movements of the planets and culminated, as planned, with the planet Venus becoming visible as it set in the darkening western sky. What was not planned was that heavy clouds should part to reveal the planet as the ritual ended; and what was not guaranteed was that the first sight of the waxing sickle Moon should also prove to be visible alongside Venus as both celestial bodies set. Not surprisingly, that particular ritual proved to be a resolution, a blessing and a turning-point for almost everyone who was there.

The essence of Creative Astrology lies in its insistence on experiencing astrological symbolism directly. It is an empirical method of finding out how astrological symbolism works. The essays in this collection show that this approach brings unexpected and rewarding results, not only in the personal lives of its users, but more theoretically, in people's understanding of astrological principles as well as in our perception of the 'objective' world around us.

Bibliography

Assagioli, Roberto, *Psychosynthesis*, Turnstone Press, Wellingborough, 1984

Campion, Nicholas, *An Introduction to the History of Astrology*, ISCWA, London, 1982

Drury, Neville, *The Elements of Human Potential*, Element Books, Shaftesbury, 1990

Gilchrist, Cherry, *Planetary Symbolism in Astrology*, Astrological Association, London, 1980

Greene, Liz, *The Astrology of Fate*, George Allen & Unwin, London, 1990

Ben Shimon Halevi, Z'ev, *The Way of Cabbalah*, Rider, London, 1976

Howe, Ellic, *Urania's Children: The Strange World of the Astrologers*, William Kimber, London, 1967

Lakatos, Imre, and Musgrave, Alan (eds.) *Criticism and the Growth of Knowledge*, CUP, Cambridge, 1970

Leo, Alan, *Esoteric Astrology*, London, 1913

Martin, Graham Dunstan, *Shadows in the Cave*, Penguin Arkana, Harmondsworth, 1990

Pottenger, Maritha, *Encounter Astrology*, T.I.A. Publications, Los Angeles, 1978

Rowan, John, *Ordinary Ecstasy: Humanistic Psychology in Action*, Routledge & Kegan Paul, London, 1976

Schermer, Barbara, *Astrology Alive!*, Aquarian, Wellingborough, 1989

Szasz, Thomas S., *The Myth of Mental Illness*, Secker & Warburg, London, 1962

Thomas, Keith, *Religion and the Decline of Magic*, Penguin, Harmondsworth, 1970

═══ 1 ═══

SYMBOLS, GUIDED IMAGERY AND CLIENT-CENTRED ASTROLOGY

Babs Kirby

Commentary

This volume begins with an example of the art. Babs Kirby presents a psychological journey into Saturn's realm, followed by the discoveries of some travellers who have been there. It is a journey that readers with or without a knowledge of astrology can try for themselves, and it will give experienced astrologers some idea of the guidelines to be followed when constructing a journey of this sort. One advantage of guided imagery rather than more demonstrative expressions of symbolism such as painting or role-playing, as Babs points out, is that it respects the enquirer's privacy. The enquirer is enabled to explore him/herself at an individual pace and at a level of intensity which suits him or her personally. This is non-invasive and supportive of each person's ability to structure his or her life meaningfully, rather than simply to believe someone else's interpretation of it. Unlike the conventional chart reading, power is placed in the hands of the enquirer rather than in those of the authoritative expert who interprets their chart to them. The examples which follow the exercise, of Saturn journeys already undertaken, make lively reading for both beginner and expert astrologer alike.

P. H. J.

Many people come to astrology in order to understand themselves better, to make sense of their lives. It is for them the beginning of a path to self-discovery. Astrology provides a framework within which we can begin to make sense of the universe and individual lives within it. My particular orientation is to try to make sense of, and find the meaning and purpose of, our own individual journeys through life.

I want to examine how both astrological principles and guided imagery are symbolic ways of understanding life and to demonstrate how to use guided imagery with astrological principles. I will discuss the advantages of using this technique to explore the natal chart over more conventional chart interpretation and show its application as both therapeutic and pedagogical.

Conventional chart interpretation, from a therapeutic point of view, could be argued to be highly intrusive and invasive of the client. Clients are generally being told things about themselves rather than being assisted in discovering their own truths. Very often the astrologer will interpret in a way the client does not recognise and cannot use. Some clients will simply reject what does not fit them, while others may suffer. This will to some extent depend on the power the client invests the astrologer with to know and understand them. In either situation astrology is tarnished. Astrology as a language to understand our process and to give greater meaning to our lives has been lost. In interpreting a chart the astrologer–client relationship is often not considered very important, yet it is an essential component of the interaction if the interpretation of the astrological symbolism is to be useful and helpful. I want to show that when using guided imagery, we, as potential clients, in effect interpret our own chart. We are led to understand it for ourselves, and this process leads us by its very nature automatically to an understanding that is at an appropriate level and relevant to where we are at that time within ourselves.

18

Let me define guided imagery in the sense I am using it. Guided imagery is an imaginal journey which we, as participants, follow, where certain related symbols and symbolic scenarios are presented by the person leading the journey. It is like being in a waking dream, and in a similar way to dreams our guided imagery journeys contain simultaneously many levels of meaning.

From a guided imagery journey we discover a personal set of symbols that illuminate for us the personal meaning of the abstract astrological symbols. Before we examine the advantages of understanding astrological symbols in this way let me say a little on a theoretical level about symbolism and outline the concept of the left and right brain hemispheres and what they govern. The left brain governs our thinking, rational and logical nature and the right brain governs our feeling, imaginative and non-rational nature.

To understand symbolism we have to plug into the right brain's function. Symbolism is not rational or logical – and neither is astrology, and yet astrology is virtually entirely taught in a left brain way.

Astrological symbols are extremely deep and complex, with many levels and layers of meaning. There is no limit to our understanding of what the planets can symbolise. It grows and changes and in this sense astrological symbolism is alive and has a life of its own.

From this we may think that a symbol is intrinsically complicated, but virtually anything can act as a symbol. All words are in fact symbols, and can have a fairly literal meaning or a more complex symbolic meaning. A doorway can be a straightforward literal thing, or can be symbolic, can suggest a transition – something beyond – something to be entered or not. Similarly a flower is just a flower or a symbol of love and much more. Interflora advertise with the phrase 'Say it with flowers' and suggest that different flowers will say different things. This is an everyday and accepted use of symbols. Symbols have both universal meanings that most people will understand plus personal and individual meanings.

19

Symbols have many functions and I will touch on three that Assagioli discusses in his book *Psychosynthesis*. He sees symbols as firstly being accumulators of a dynamic psychological charge. Most of us will easily recognise this, that certain symbols are highly charged for us and act as containers of powerful psychological energy. An example would be spiders or snakes, which universally tend to act as a highly charged symbol, but many other things can work in this way for specific individuals.

A second function of symbols is that of transformers of psychological energy. For example befriending spiders or snakes changes a lot on a deeper level too.

A third function is that of conductors or channels of psychological energies, thus bringing to the surface some of the issues a symbol encapsulates and represents in a person.

Symbols in all these functions have most important and useful therapeutic and educational functions. The sequence of a symbol is that of attracting psychological energies, storing them, transforming them and then utilising them for some purpose particularly for the important one of integration. Another function and use of symbols is their effect upon the unconscious. To quote Assagioli directly:

> Symbols can be visualised and this sets into motion unconscious psychological processes. This is an effective means for the transformation of the unconscious. To address the unconscious in logical terms in not particularly effective. In order to reach the unconscious, as in reaching any person, we have to speak in its own terms. One should attempt to use the mode in which the unconscious normally operates, which is by way of symbols. Besides the fact that symbols in themselves have integrating value, in other words, integrate psychic material within the unconscious, the technique of consciously utilising symbols by visualising them achieves a further integration between the conscious and unconscious elements of the personality, and between the

20

logical mind and the non-logical aspects of the person. Jung has said that symbols are transformers of psychic energy.

Therefore what we can expect is that by presenting certain symbols to the unconscious of a person, there will be set in motion certain unconscious forces that will bring about outer change. A process is set off that may take considerable time to unfold, but that eventually will manifest in some outer change. This is of course a process of growth going on all the time in everyone to a greater or lesser extent.

When we use symbols in guided imagery we are setting off a quite powerful process, and what is set off may be felt consciously for several days. Dreams may contain fragments relating to the process that has been triggered and inner psychic material will wend its way to consciousness and greater integration.

With a guided imagery journey written to evoke a particular planetary principle a fairly tightly controlled and related set of symbols and symbolic scenarios are presented that will deliberately trigger a succession of images surrounding this principle.

There are two different processes operating for someone who embarks on this journey. The first, which is therapeutic, is that a process is set off in the unconscious which leads to an increase in self-awareness and a step along the path to individuation.

The second, which is educational, is to understand what the particular planetary principle means to us and how it operates within us and our life. By being in a group and sharing the images from the journey we can also understand how others' experience of the same principle is different and relate that to the different placements in their charts.

So that this chapter should not just be theory, and so that you can 'know' on a different level what I am talking about, I am going to give you an example of a guided imagery journey on Saturn's principle. To go on this journey yourself you need someone to read it to you very slowly, leaving pauses as indicated, for your imagination to have free rein. You can also tape it for yourself and then proceed to go on the journey. I sometimes play music when I take people on this journey, and have made a continuous tape of Holst's 'Saturn' from *The Planets*. I start with a simple relaxation exercise, and if possible I have participants lie down. Anyone who tends to fall asleep in these exercises should, I would suggest, stay sitting in a comfortable position with both feet on the floor and eyes closed.

Before you embark on this journey I would like to say a few more things about guided imagery.

It is a safe yet powerful way of getting in touch with your own inner self. You set your own limits and will only dip down as far as is safe for you – very much as in dreams. In this case it is a waking dream that is being guided to evoke the principle of Saturn for you to discover your relationship to Saturn's symbolism.

When doing imagery it is important not to censor your images. If you cut them off you may cut yourself off entirely from your imaginal flow. Try to move with them, change them and adapt them if you wish, but do not censor them or you will lose your thread and your images may dry up. In work like this it is important to feel safe. The safer the situation you are in the deeper you will allow yourself to go down into unconscious material.

While on a guided imagery journey you need to use your right brain entirely and to switch off your left brain. Do not think about where Saturn is in your chart or try to analyse the journey. Let go of all preconceptions you have about Saturn and just allow whatever comes into your imagination. Allow your imagination a free rein. I will discuss the journey and what its symbolism means later.

Like dreams, the contents of guided imagery journeys can evaporate very rapidly from conscious recall, and for this reason I recommend writing your journey down immediately you surface from it, before you speak with anyone else. In a workshop situation I would always make it clear that this record is private and for yourself, and it is up to you how much or how little of your journey you later share. This is important in terms of what you allow yourself to image too, as, if you feel everything has to be subsequently shared, you will censor any images you are not comfortable with sharing.

Make sure you are physically comfortable and warm enough as body temperatures often drop when lying still. First I will go through a simple relaxation exercise, and then on to a guided imagery journey on Saturn.

Focus on your feet, be aware of any tension in them, and relax, let them go loose. (pause)

Focus on your calves and knees, be aware of any tension in them, and let go of it, relax. (pause)

Focus on your thighs and buttocks, be aware of any tension in them, and relax. Feel how heavy your legs are when you let the tension go. (pause)

Focus on you stomach, chest and back, be aware of any tension, and relax, let go of it. Feel your back on the ground and yourself supported. Let yourself sink into the ground. Let your breath become slow and steady and reach right down into your stomach. (pause)

Focus on your shoulders, arms and hands, be aware of any tension in them, and let go of it, relax. Let your hands, arms and shoulders go limp, and feel how heavy your arms are when you stop holding them, they are being supported right now. (pause)

Focus on your neck and jaw, be aware of any tension in them, and let go of it, relax. Your head is being supported, your neck can let go. Let your jaw hang loose. Relax. (pause)

Focus on your face, your eyes, you nose, your mouth, lips, tongue, your scalp, and relax, let go of any tension, let your whole face go loose, even floppy. Relax. (pause)

Take a few deep breaths, and let go of any remaining tensions, let your mind become clear. (pause)

I want you to imagine that you are a mole. (short pause)
You're small and furry.
You live underground. (short pause)
The earth around you is cool and damp and pleasant-smelling.
Be aware of its texture and consistency. (short pause)
You're digging a passage. (short pause)
What is yours like? (pause)
Is it straight? (short pause) or bending? (short pause)
Do you move quickly? (short pause) or slowly? (short pause)
What is your direction? (long pause)
You come to a boulder. (short pause)
It blocks your way forward. (short pause)
How do you deal with this? (pause)
Can you find a way forward and continue? (long pause)
You are actually a part of a mole colony that has existed for thousands of years. (short pause)
Imagine how you all relate as a colony now. (very long pause)
There are spoken and unspoken rules of how to behave and what is acceptable. Imagine what they are. (long pause)
There are even moles elected to uphold the spoken rules. (short pause)
How do you fit in? (pause)
How constrained do you feel by the rules? (pause)
How protected do you feel by the rules? (pause)
Do you betray anything of yourself to live in this colony? (pause)
Within the colony is a very old and wise mole. (short pause)
She/he has a home and you go to it. (pause)
What does she/he look like? (pause)
What is their home like? (pause)
You can ask them any question and they will give you an answer. (short pause)
Be aware of what you want to ask. (long pause)

Now ask your question. (short pause)

And hear their answer. (pause)

You say goodbye and leave their home, coming back along the tunnel you've already made. (short pause)

You go back to where you were in the beginning. (short pause)

When you are ready, open your eyes and gradually come back into the room.

I will now explain the symbolism in this journey. I chose an underground creature, the mole, to conjure up a strong positive relationship to the earth and because a mole has, quite literally, to dig its own path. It is all your own work and endeavour and how easy or difficult this is for you shows something of how the Saturn principle operates within you. Some people imagine heavy clay soil, which is very difficult to move through and it is slow, tedious work to get anywhere, while others have a light loamy soil that they move through pretty effortlessly, something we can all recognise as how things seem for us.

The direction is important, whether you have a sense of direction, of knowing where you are headed for, or not, and how directly you are heading for it. Saturn's principle has a lot to do with our direction, our goals, our ambitions.

Then there is the obstacle. Obvious Saturn stuff, but how you deal with it is extremely relevant and reflects how obstacles are experienced within you right now, your current intrinsic attitude towards them, and how thwarted or otherwise you feel by them; whether you are challenged and spurred on by them or easily defeated.

Some people's obstacles are huge too, and others imagine small obstacles they can deal with easily, again showing something of where they are at with the Saturn principle.

Which way you get around your obstacle is also symbolically important. While this cannot be rigidly interpreted and depends on individuals, as a guide, going around the obstacle to the left is a yin, feminine-based resolution, representing using the right brain to resolve obstacles, while going to the right represents using the left brain and using a masculine, logical, rational approach to get out of dilemmas. Going underneath the obstacle suggests digging down within oneself for solutions, possibly into one's psychological depths while going over the obstacle suggests going up into the intellect or possibly spiritual realms for solutions. This is not to say there are not other creative and ingenious ways of dealing with the obstacle, which we will look at later, but these are the main solutions I have met.

The next part is showing Saturn within society, as the rules that are meant to make the wheels of social life run smoothly and protect us, yet can also restrict and limit us. How well we fit into society and what price, if any, we pay to fit in. The rules you imagine are always relevant and the way of life of the colony. It will show something of how adjusted you are to being a part of our larger society.

Some people will always set themselves outside of the norm, of mainstream society. Some will kick against it. Their own natal Saturn may be in difficult aspect to other chart factors and they cannot internalise and incorporate its principle and will subsequently experience their Saturn as outside of themselves. The police, authorities, bureaucracies and institutions are all potentially on the end of negative Saturn projections and treated with hostility and fear and subsequently these very aspects of society do constrict and thwart them. They have not established an inner reconciliation with this principle. Their difficulty is probably rooted in their early relationship to their father and often involves a fair amount of painful introspection to illuminate and redeem.

You can also get people who are overattached to the Saturn principle, very safe and comfortable within the rules as if the rules were the absolute truth. They are not: they are just an aspect of society's functioning that we have to adjust to in order to operate within it. These people may be unduly restricted in themselves by Saturnian reality which will

26

block them from realising essential parts of themselves. These people tend to have a very hard time with the outer planets, which I do think represent different truths, and which do not respect Saturnian reality at all.

The final part is to connect you back into the most positive attribute of Saturn within yourself, the part which has the wisdom of experience.

For some people there is a clear connection to their father here, for others it is a special person, for some no one they recognise. Whatever, it is, it will be an aspect of yourself that you can turn to. The home will occasionally describe the house placement of natal Saturn.

The two examples of a Saturn journey that follow come from two participants of an ongoing guided imagery group, in which they went on a different journey each week for each of the planets. Both were in individual therapy as well. The situation was a relatively safe one, so they had greater access to deeper inner material, plus the safety of somewhere to take it to further if they needed to.

This is Esther's Saturn journey as she recorded it and the relevant planets in her natal chart are shown in Figure 1. I have added, in brackets, the astrological significators that I think she speaks from.

Digging the tunnel is a bit boring, but I'm not really concentrating very hard (Sun conjunct Saturn conjunct Neptune in Libra). There's some clay in the soil and I'm using it to decorate the walls – formal stuff like doric columns, only two-dimensional. Sense of splendour or old formality in the designs. I'm not very serious about this tunnel (Saturn square Uranus), it's something I have to do and I'm trying to make it more fun. It's a very beautiful tunnel (Libra). I'm quite enjoying it because I'm being a bit 'naughty', not just tunnelling but playing; I've no clear idea where I'm going and it's not really important (Saturn square Uranus, Mercury conjunct Ascendant, Saturn conjunct Neptune in the 12th house). When I get to the boulder

27

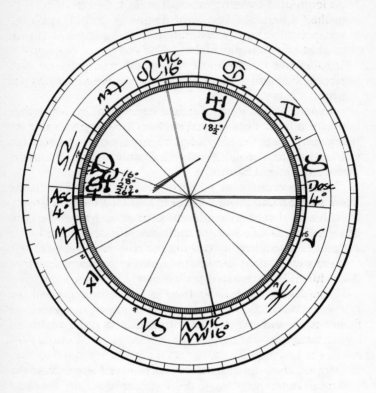

Fig. 1 Esther   Data withheld for confidentiality

I stop and have a rest and then start doing a painting on it. Perhaps it's abstract but I think of clouds and sky so perhaps it's of the outside. Again there's an idea of formality. I stay painting my boulder. Then the music changes and I know I'm part of this ancient line of moles with a history. I have a picture of gladiatorial moles, of tradition, battle and craftsmanship. Really it's a bit pompous but I'm smiling at the idea of moley legions under a standard.

When I think about it the place where I am is a vast

28

underground dwelling-place, rather like a church with vaulted roofs and lots of niches and nooks and places set apart. It's not gloomy and there's a feeling of peaceful co-existence (Saturn in Libra). The order and rules give a sense of freedom in a way. Everyone has his or her own place and knows where they belong – a firm base to go out from.

Rules – well what you know and need to live with other people. I don't find them a problem. I may have to give up my playfulness to be here. I don't think so though because I go off and paint boulders when I should be digging tunnels (Saturn square Uranus).

There's an old wise mole, I look at him and he has glasses on. He's my dad, serious but with twinkling eyes, he knows such a lot. I start to cry. His room is filled with books, old ones in tones of terracotta and brown. I feel very at home here. The books are all around the walls up to the ceiling, there's wood here and it's comfortable (Saturn in Libra). I ask him if I can stay here with him and he replies that I can as long as I need to. I stay there.

Esther is someone who is, if anything, overattached to the Saturn principle. This journey was particularly important for her as she had positive contact with her father (who had died some time ago in reality). At that time she had very little access within herself to positive connections to him.

Next is Sally's journey with the relevant planets in her natal chart shown in Figure 2.

I'm a mole and I like being in the dark surrounded by the dark earth. I hate the light. I like to be surrounded all over by the slight pressure of damp, dark earth.

I'm making a passage away from the surface; I hate the surface (Saturn in Sagittarius in the 9th house). Every so often I stop and sleep and rest and feel replenished by the security of knowing I'm surrounded by the earth. My progress is slow but I'm not particularly going anywhere.

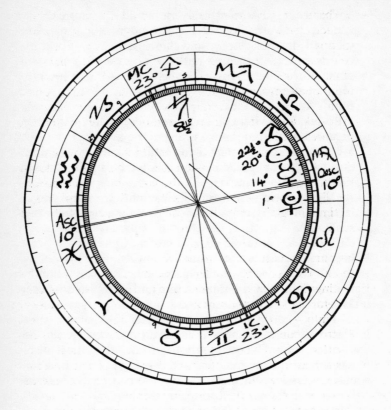

Fig. 2 Sally   Data withheld for confidentiality

There's a boulder. It won't move, it's solid (Saturn square Pluto). I push against it with my head and it won't move at all. I think about going under it but then think it may go on for ever. Then I think it would be better to go up, but I hate going up. I hate the light. I won't go up. Then I think I'll eat it. Then I realise boulders can't stop me. Boulders stop stupid light beings but not us moles! So I just say a few of the old spells and the boulder withers away.

That's our mission. As moles our whole life and existence is dedicated to destroying all that holds up the light world (Saturn in Sagittarius in the 9th house). I'm part of a colony and we work as we have always worked, separately, alone, towards one goal. There is one rule, to destroy the foundation of the world of the light beings (Saturn square Pluto). We all know this rule. It is born in us, it is our lives. We work alone knowing that we work together towards the final destruction.

I am called to the place of our king. The place is all dark. I do not see him but I know he's there. I know the time has come to destroy the last columns supporting the light world. I ask him 'Is it time?' He says 'Yes, it is time.' I go. I am pleased it is time to deal the last blow.

This journey, with all its intensity and drama, is virtually pure Saturn square Pluto. This square was being set off by transiting Saturn at the time of this journey. It took place a little before her Saturn return as transiting Saturn squared her natal Pluto – hence all the destruction of light beings. There is a strong counterbalance emerging to what was beneath the surface of all the idealisation, belief, 'light' as it were, of a 9th house Sagittarius Saturn. People with Saturn Pluto contacts will often attempt to stay on the surface of life but will sooner or later get pulled in and down into darker levels. As her Saturn return approached she was poised at this point of initiation into a deeper level of herself.

Here are a few details from other people's journeys.

Someone with Saturn conjunct the IC asked her wise person if she would find her security.

Someone with Saturn in Virgo in the 12th house found digging the tunnel so difficult that when he reached the obstacle he heaved a huge sigh of relief and sat down, using it as a backrest. Here we have a second person with Saturn in the 12th not experiencing the obstacle as an obstacle in the conventional way or feeling any need to get by it.

31

Someone else with Saturn trine Uranus dynamited her obstacle.

As you will see, this is rich material that could be explored further and offers a direct pathway into exploring the psyche. A journey can be understood on many different levels. In a workshop situation, where participants may not know each other and it is not a particularly safe space to explore one's inner world, a guided imagery journey is an extremely safe way to explore oneself. It is an inner private experience, in which participants can share as little or as much of their journeys as they feel willing to. In this situation I would emphasise that journeys should not be interpreted further, but that astrological significators for the content of the journey can be suggested. When combining an astrological understanding with personal growth there are one or two land-mines to navigate. One is that astrology can be an extremely detached and impersonal way of understanding life, and when you combine it with guided imagery participants are going to get much closer to potentially painful inner material. Anyone sharing new material is vulnerable to someone who is over-detached (as many astrologers are) interpreting their journey with hobnail boots. For this reason I always just use the journeys for educational purposes in workshop situations, while emphasising that the material is still useful from a therapeutic point of view. It is something that participants can explore further in a counselling or therapy situation.

In an ongoing group situation the same caution does not apply, and the journeys can be explored in considerable depth, offering a very rich experience for personal growth and enhanced astrological understanding.

What I particularly like about guided imagery, is that it is a technique that reveals a person to themselves. As in a dream, that contains many levels of meaning and can be understood by the dreamer on whatever level they are ready for, so guided imagery gives us instant access to deeper levels of ourselves to understand on whatever level we are ready to understand it on. The images can be interpreted further, but they do not have to be. Someone with a Moon–Saturn conjunction visualised on a Moon-guided imagery journey a very bare, unpeopled, snow-covered landscape. This is something he at the time could easily see as Moon–Saturn. He did not see it as bleak, or cold, or lonely; he was comfortable and at home in this landscape. Later in life he may see this time as more emotionally barren than he does right now, but it is his to connect to as he is ready.

With guided imagery you enable a person to explore themselves at their pace. A situation is set up whereby a person is held within a certain framework to speak their chart.

With all the journeys I have written, although they are written to evoke a particular planetary principle, anything that resonates will also come through. For instance, on a Moon journey, as well as the Moon and aspects to the Moon being imaged, any planets in Cancer or the 4th house may also be evoked. With a Saturn journey, transiting Saturn will often come through. (I have written other journeys to evoke specific transits too.) These journeys always reveal where you are currently at with this principle, so if you were to do the same journey later, your images would change to reflect the changes in you. Sometimes very immediate current stimuli can affect your images, like simply being too cold and imaging snow. As was stated earlier guided imagery journeys will always contain a mixture of levels, some of the images being stimulated by recent current events and some describing long-term underlying issues.

This type of work empowers the client, whereas conventional astrological interpretation can so easily disempower. This is a thorny area that all astrologers have to grapple with in some way or another. In many ways the whole issue is circumvented by creating ways that clients can discover for themselves what a particular planetary principle means to them, and having explored it in this way they will really 'know' what it means to them and can draw on this knowledge at any time, it is an instinctual, right-brained knowledge, as opposed to an intellectual, left-brained knowledge.

In particular, guided imagery is useful for those who want to understand their own inner world in terms of their chart. It is a powerful tool for grounding inner experiences in astrological symbolism and is a very personal way to know astrology. As most people come to astrology for a deeper personal understanding of themselves, guided imagery on the astrological principles offers a route to understanding not only their psyche, but the relationship between their psyche and their natal chart.

Bibliography

Assagioli, M. D., Roberto, *Psychosynthesis*, Turnstone Press, Wellingborough, 1984

Ernst, Sheila, and Goodison, Lucy, *In Our Own Hands*, The Women's Press, London, 1981

Gallegos, Eligio Stephen, and Rennick, Teresa, *Inner Journeys*, Turnstone Press, Wellingborough, 1984

Gilchrist, Cherry, *Planetary Symbolism in Astrology*, Saros Foundation, Astrological Association of Great Britain, 1980

Greene, Liz, *Saturn*, Samuel Weiser, New York, 1976

Hand, Robert, *Horoscope Symbols*, Para Research, Massachusetts, 1981.

═══ 2 ═══

ASTROLOGY
PSYCHODRAMA

Hans Planje

Commentary

Hans Planje takes psychological exploration out of the realm
of private fantasy and into the semi-public area of the group.
As he points out, astrology was not originally concerned
with the individual at all, but with the collective. The
earliest personal horoscopes which we have are those for
monarchs, which were surely drawn up for the monarch in
his or her role as representative of the nation. Astrological
principles permeate the whole of existence, not just the
individual psyche, and in the three levels of astrodrama
(astrological psychodrama) which he describes, Hans returns
to the original role of theatre as well as of astrology; to put a
community into harmony with the massive archetypes which
govern the lives of us all. The various exercises which are
described here will be of interest to many groups and group
leaders, and his comments on the mysterious relationship
between dramatic enactment of the elements of astrology, in
an astrodrama group or indeed in ritual, and their strange
propensity to manifest unexpectedly in the environment at
the time, will give many astrologers food for thought.

P. H. J.

'As above, so below' is one of the oldest sayings on which astrology is based. It tells us that what we can observe when we look up to the sky is also present on earth: the cosmos is reflected in man. Perhaps we could say that the astrology of the last centuries changed this saying into: 'As above, forget below', because we have developed the 'above' – our mind – extremely well in the last few hundred years, but have lost the connection with our 'below' – our body and our emotions. We have lost contact with our roots and with the roots of astrology. Fortunately a reversal of this one-sided development is now underway and in so-called New Age thinking the human being is seen again as a unity of body, soul and mind together. Astrodrama also is a method in which the 'above' and the 'below' are connected and man is approached in a holistic way.

Dane Rudhyar wrote that every astrology represents the culture of the time in which it exists. Today we live in a world in which soul, body and mind are excessively separated from each other. As astrologers we can notice this for instance in the development and spread of various techniques, new systems and new methods, which have become possible with the arrival of the computer. These overload us with more and more information and possibilities, but actually take us further away from ourselves.

A Bit of History

The conventional history of astrology says that it came into existence in ancient Babylon, where wise men and priests observed the movements of the starry sky and made careful observations. In later ages, slowly and surely, connections were made between these observations and developments and events on earth.

I'm convinced that the roots of astrology are much deeper and that its development dates from a much older source. Before the rationalism of Aristotle and the monotheism of

36

Judaism, the world looked very different. God was not the Father in heaven who passed his messages through the priests. God, or rather the gods, became manifest everywhere in nature: in plants, in animals, in natural phenomena and in human beings. This manifestation in human beings was mainly through feminine expression. The matriarchy of the pre-Aryan age had a very comprehensive consciousness of the universe which was rather different from our present consciousness. In the pantheistic thinking of God-is-in-all a separation of 'above' and 'below' was not possible. There was no clear difference between men and nature. In this time of gods and goddesses everything was animated and the cosmos was not discovered and studied by calculating it or by making objective analyses. It was not necessary to study the movements of Mars to understand his influence. Mars was not a strange object somewhere in the cosmos: he was on earth, in fire, in the wild animals, in the hottest spices, in the shout of the hunter, in the body of the human being, directly perceptible and clearly tangible.

Even in the time of Ptolemy, in the second century after Christ, the planets were not seen as symbols for or the residence of the gods. They were seen as lively gods in men themselves. The rich Greek mythology may be a clear example of this. The rise of the patriarchal religions and the rationalism of the later Greeks separated us more and more from nature and the planets. And parallel to this development astrology concentrated more and more on the individual being and less on the collective.

Originally astrology was not concerned with the individual. It was completely for the use of the collective and was meant to rule society as well as possible. Therefore 'techniques' like ritual, dance, prayer, meditation and art were used. This was a time in which people were taught to experience the planets in the body and in the heart.

The shamans, medicine men, witches, druids and priests were the holy leaders of the different societies, who knew how to contact the cosmic forces and how to handle them.

But when we began to develop our individuality, we also started losing our feeling for the collective in our striving after personality. Analogous to this process, astrology developed into what it has now become. The contributions of patriarchal culture to society are of course enormous and we have made a big step in evolution, but in this process we lost contact with the cosmos.

In the social commotion and changes of the 1960s, experiential astrology was rediscovered. The hippies' desire to turn back to nature was for many a source of inspiration. The spiritual community of Findhorn in Scotland began to use important astronomical configurations for rituals and celebrations to receive planetary energies and direct them for collective purposes. Both in Europe and in the States individual astrologers began to develop astrodrama independently from one another, by making astrological knowledge experiential and practical. The spirit of this movement remains in spite of the 'me' generation and the yuppification of Western society.

When we take a look at the astrological calendars of New Age magazines, we find more and more astrodrama activities. Astrologers started to reconnect people with the cosmic energies of the elements, the zodiac and the planets. Anyone who is searching for the substance of life, perhaps has the feeling of missing something or feels that astrology is more than knowledge, calculations and techniques, *and* who is able to open himself to wider possibilities, can learn through astrodrama more about astrology, but mainly about himself.

Astrodrama

The purpose of astrodrama is to rediscover connections: the connection between the head and the heart and the connections between one another, between the planets and the life-forces in ourselves and around us. It is not meant to reject or exclude other or newly developed methods. It just

38

tries to fill up and complete the proliferation of individual energies with a holistic relation to the universe. It is astrology in its purest form, an astrology that we can use always and everywhere, whenever we need it.

Now I should say something about the 'techniques' of astrodrama. I don't think that the possibilities of astrodrama can be described under one collective methodic principle. The quintessence of astrodrama is to make the archetypal energies, which in astrological jargon we call the four elements, the signs of the zodiac and the planets, visible and lively, without restricting the archetypal multifariousness of their expression. Music, sound, singing, dance, movement, (role) play, theatre, visualisation, guided imagery, meditation and working with rituals are all possible mediums through which to make astrological principles perceivable and expressible. Apart from using your voice, it is also possible to express them with the help of drawing and painting materials, needle and thread, modelling clay or in the form of a story or poem.

Bio-energetics, voice dialogue, yoga, massage, and other techniques can also be considered as forms of astrodrama, provided that they are placed in an astrological framework. A yoga exercise can be specially meant to strengthen your earth energy, a massage can help you to let go of things (Neptune) or a chakra exercise can be directed to strengthen your vitality – that is, your Sun energy.

First I will say something about my personal background and relate the following part of this essay to my own way of using astrology and astrodrama.

In my job as youth worker in the 1970s, I had already experienced the need to make all kinds of processes clearly visible, tangible and perceptible and bring the people with whom I worked into direct contact with their inner emotions. The best way to realise this was by using role-play and similar techniques. At that time I started a psychodrama training at the German Moreno Institute for Psychodrama, Sociometry and Group Psychotherapy. From the very beginning of this training, I was fascinated by the possibilities of its connection with astrology and I felt the power of healing by the combination of ASTROlogy and psychoDRAMA, which I called ASTRODRAMA.

Different Levels of Astrodrama

Astrodrama can be experienced on different levels: playful and artistic, research-oriented or pedagogic, or psychological and therapeutic. Those three fields are not strictly delimited, but overlap each other. In a simple role-play for example, you will always meet a part of yourself. As soon as you realise this and start to reflect, a therapeutic process begins. I'll try to describe the quintessence of each of these fields and give some examples.

The first level, which for convenience I called 'playful and artistic', brings us into contact with the cosmic energies of the four elements, the signs of the zodiac and the planets. It teaches us to look with an astrological eye at ourselves and the world around us and for instance to discriminate fire energy from earth energy. With the help of simple exercises the participants are brought into contact with a certain energy and at first it is important to watch what happens, how your body reacts, how moods, feelings and atmospheres change, and how your surroundings are influenced by this.

A nice example for this is the so-called keyword circle. The participants are asked to free-associate to an astrological concept. One after another the participants say a word which in their opinion is related to the chosen concept. It is important that a quick tempo is created in the circle, so that the unconscious associative mind is activated and intuition flows more easily. Another important thing is that no statement that is mentioned by one of the participants is wrong. If someone says 'cold' for the Fire element, this probably says something about his momentary feeling towards the Fire element, or he may be expressing something that is

40

valid for the whole group. It is of course possible to extend this variety with sounds or movements that match the astrological concept in question.

And now we enter into the field of physical expression. Body language is one of the clearest expressions of astrological principles, provided that you understand this language. We all have an image of the person who underlines what he is saying with vehement gestures. This behaviour could be seen as an expression of Mercury or the Gemini sign, or possibly of Mars; it depends on how he expresses himself *and* what we see and feel ourselves. But how do we recognise Venus, and in which attitudes do Neptune or Pluto express themselves?

In some branches of Sufism the concept of planetary walk was used. The idea is to connect the planets with our body while we are walking. By concentrating, being aware of certain parts of our body and adjusting our physical attitude, we can activate energy from these parts and express this in our way of walking. When you concentrate for instance on your hips and put them forward while you are walking and make your steps a bit longer than usual, you'll activate the energy of Jupiter on a physical level. Visualising a thick belly, making wide shoulders and puffing up your cheeks a little bit, will help you to enter deeper into the Jovian energy. And see what happens when you walk in this energy through a busy shopping street . . .

Another way to work physically with the planetary energies is by imagining and playing roles, as it happens in the 'Planetary Ball'. Every participant chooses to represent a planet by using disguise and greasepaint. In the ball the planets meet and interact, in order to explore their different expressions and energetic relations.

Now we come to the second level of using astrodrama, which I called 'research-oriented or pedagogic' and in which the exploration and training of different levels and expressions of the planetary energies is central. The point here is to learn how you yourself can actively handle the planetary concepts.

Astrology is not just something we learn to help other people or to make headway against the limits of our own chart. Substantially it is an instrument for personal trans-formation, because the limits we experience in our natal chart are not limits in fact, but only in perception. When we make real contact with the archetypes of the planets, we train ourselves by means of their qualities at the same time and so discover the essence of the planetary gods within ourselves. As human beings we have access to all information in collective human experiences. As spiritually inspired living inhabitants of the universe, we form part of all of its units.

Experiential astrology helps us to discover the pure essence of the signs of the zodiac and the planets, to make ourself familiar with and to master it, so that we can use it when we need it. Consciousness of the collective level of astrology gives us the ability to have at our disposal both a personal and a collective way of dealing with life's problems and of discovering its multitudinous joys.

Practically, it means that in the first place we learn to know and recognise the planetary forces, within ourselves as well as around us. We have to develop a feeling for the various levels and expressions through which these manifest. We can see how the archetypal forces are used and expressed differently by every human being, not least because we learn to recognise our own possibilities and restrictions.

A clear example of working with special energies is in a group. The leader activates a certain energy either by using music, sound or movement, or through a visualisation or a breathing exercise. At first this energy is activated in everybody personally, assuming they are open to the exercise; but at the same time it also comes into existence as group energy. Every participant will express this energy in a different way, have different body sensations and experience a different state of mind. The created group energy can be very strong and quite often it happens that while working with Saturn energy for instance, a boss or another official person comes in to arrange, control or forbid something.

Mercury energy seems not only to inspire the participants to start talking and exchanging information, but also to activate telephones and doorbells. Uranian energy influences the electricity, and often strange noises start coming into the group from outside. By watching each other and sharing experiences a wider, more differentiated picture of the planet in question is developed and for everybody possibilities are created of getting more insight into one's own way of dealing with and managing the restrictions of this special energy. Finally through knowing your own difficulties and imperfections, you will also learn to understand and accept others.

And now we are touching the field that I called 'psychological and therapeutic' before (sorry, I don't know any better expressions). For it will be clear that the borders between personal experience and therapy are hard to draw, and that the effect and intensity of the different forms of astrodrama will not be restricted only to one level. Every experiential working with astrology brings about the inevitable meeting with parts of yourself. It also depends on the intended aims and on what someone is able and willing to pick up and work on at that special moment, how far it fits within the scope of the class, workshop, school or therapy setting.

Working in this 'level' of astrodrama requires a therapeutically trained group leader, because in this field it is important to be able to analyse the themes touched on by the relevant planet (s) at greater depth, and if necessary correct by means of therapeutic intervention. As I said before, for me this therapeutic background is psychodrama, in which I trained at the Moreno Institute in West Germany at the end of the 1970s.

Psychodrama

Psychodrama is a group therapy method developed by J. L. Moreno in which drama – the action – is central. This happens by means of role-play, which is staged by the protagonist – the player of the leading part. The antagonists – the fellow players chosen by the protagonist – give the protagonist feedback from their roles. In this way actual existing situations of conflict can be played and worked out, in order to help the protagonist to get more insight into the way he or she handles and manages this theme, into what he or she is projecting and what he or she evokes in other people. These themes can of course be astrological themes, which are experienced as problematic by the protagonist. In addition it won't be very difficult for a skilled astrologer to reduce the themes offered – if the protagonist doesn't know anything about astrology – to astrological symbolism, and give it a place in his or her chart. There are some specific psychodrama techniques that are especially effective in therapeutic working with groups or with individuals (in which case we speak about monodrama).

I will now discuss some of these techniques. In the first place, as I mentioned before, there is role-play. The main function is to learn to put yourself in the place of somebody else, other situations or objects, through which you can get insight by looking at your situation from other points of view. At the same time other people's rendering of their own role experiences give the protagonist important feedback.

In role-play the exchange of roles is an important technique, because the protagonist is not only acting in one role, but in two complementary different roles. By means of role change the protagonist and antagonist each play out the conflict inside themselves as well. The role change into the role of relation partner makes the protagonist the subject and initiator of his or her reactions. Back in his or her own role the protagonist becomes the object and recipient of his or her own actions. This leads not only to emotional agitation and abreaction of the affect by each participant, but moreover to an integrating confrontation of the two participants, with an abreaction and inner resolution of the conflict. A better mutual perception and insight into

44

someone else often makes it just easier to deal with the conflict in reality, too.

Another important technique is doubling. This means that the protagonist gets help from someone behind him, who supports him during the role-play in his confrontation with difficult or otherwise inaccessible themes, who gives him the feeling of not being alone and the courage to continue. The doubler also has the function of verbalising, repeating and invigorating the emotions that he experiences in his identification with the protagonist and which the protagonist might not express for fear, shame or because they are unconscious. This technique is very often used by the therapist, but it could also be done by someone from the group, who would accompany the protagonist during the whole game, especially in extremely emotional, fearful or painful role-plays.

A special doubling technique is what is known as ambivalence-doubling or shadow-doubling. In this case at least two auxiliary persons are needed, each representing one side of a conflicting theme, usually the positive and the negative side, or rather the aspects of the theme experienced by the protagonist as positive and negative. Both persons stand and walk left and right of the protagonist and behave like different parts of his or her mind, in which the pros and cons of the conflict alternate. They both speak only with the one in the middle and they are not allowed to discuss directly with each other. In this way they can help the protagonist to get through to the different aspects of the theme, its possibilities and impossibilities and, not least, the corresponding emotional levels.

During the whole play it is important that the protagonist comes into and keeps in contact with his or her feelings. Therefore the therapist can intervene in the interaction and ask the protagonist to speak loudly aside and express what's going on in his or her thoughts and feelings. This helps the protagonist to get deeply in touch with emotions that might otherwise be overlooked, ignored or even denied.

45

An interesting aspect of various psychodrama techniques is the use of walking. Moreno noticed that when we are moving, we are more open, our emotions flow more easily and we are less able to block them (notice: e-motion = from motion). This principle of walking is basic to several astrodrama techniques mentioned before, for instance the planetary walks. Knowing that our body has an intelligence of its own, we can imagine that the integration of the body in the therapeutic process increases the possibilities of learning and transformation.

Finally I would like to say something about the use of rituals. Especially in the field of astrology, in which everything is connected with cycles, working with rituals has a particular place. We all know that native cultures enacted, and still enact, their rituals at times of important planetary configurations, especially those of the Sun and Moon. In our culture, however, we find a lot of ritual occasions as well, though in many cases we have lost contact with their source. Think for instance of the Christian festival days. Important planetary events, like summer or winter solstices, new or full moons, or conjunctions such as that between Saturn and Uranus in 1988, or Saturn and Neptune in 1989, are powerful energetic moments that can bring us a lot of positive energy and possibilities, assuming that we can open ourselves for it. The quintessence of a ritual is not that it has to take place in a prescribed form, but that it should be executed in a spirit of openness, respect and receptivity for the cosmic energies and with the consciousness of the bridge you are building between heaven and earth at the moment of the ritual. In that case you can give your personal form to a ritual and make use of candles for instance, of incense, singing, images, music, or anything you think that goes well with and supports this special ritual. My third astrological diary for 1990 is about the relationship between Sun and Moon and it contains meditations and visualisations for each new and full moon.

When your heart is open, miracles happen. When we attune ourselves to the cosmos and her rhythms, we open ourselves naturally. This kind of astrology is not restricted to the birth chart, but it comprises the unity of the whole universe. This is the astrology that teaches us that we are ourselves each of these planets and every sign of the zodiac. Here our individuality sinks into nothingness. If my image of Saturn is only negative, I will suffer; then astrology suffers and the world sinks further into darkness. But if my image of Saturn is positive, my Saturnian energy will meet other positive Saturnian sources, which together have a strong healing power. The richness of astrology is its universality.

Each planet has at least two different faces for each of us. One is the face that we see when we are born; it colours our perception of the world around us and creates our reality. The other is the face in its real substance, the pure energy of each planet, perfect in itself and a divine teacher and friend. When we connect ourself with the real essence of the planets, our soul will remember this and we will be able to heal ourself and the earth.

AS ABOVE, SO BELOW!

Bibliography

Moreno, J.L., *Psychodrama*, Beacon House, New York, 1956

Hans, Planje, *Astrologische Agenda*, Enschede, NL, Astrodrama, 2, 1988, –89, –90

Rudhyar, Dane, *The Planetarization of Consciousness* Wassenaar, NL, Servire, 1970

CREATIVE ASTROLOGY IN ADULT EDUCATION

Tina Whitehead

Commentary

Creative Astrology is not simply to do with psychology, even group psychology. It is a powerful aid to teaching, because in the same way that its offer of creative experience empowers the psychological enquirer, it equally empowers the student. Tina Whitehead gives a detailed account of the theoretical background to student-centred teaching of this sort, which may surprise any readers who assume that creative techniques are simply an avoidance of more formally-structured learning. This is in fact an exercise in integrating Saturn, the principle of structure, with the more dynamic elements of existence which shape our direct experience. As Tina's description of the original Creative Astrology course she ran makes clear, the tutor's theoretical understanding of the principles taught, and continual monitoring of students' progress, are an essential underpinning of the adventurous outlook encouraged in class. Nevertheless, the tutor also learns more about theory from their students' experiences, and the class soon learns to argue constructively about details of interpretation. Creative Astrology in this context follows Plato's theory that the truths about the archetypes are already known to us all, and education simply serves to draw these out. The experiment in moving geometry, the 'Dance of Venus', with which Tina's essay ends, demonstrates the intimate relationship between aesthetics, esoteric symbolism, and precise, objective measurement.

P. H. J.

Astrology is a vast and complex subject and it is not always easy to present its principles in an accessible form to students within the adult education system. Classes offered in this system attract a wide cross-section of individuals with varying educational backgrounds and reasons for attending the class. This can present the teacher with difficulties in devising and teaching a course which is appropriate for the students' needs and interests.

It is important to structure an astrology course which presents the subject in an understandable and accessible form to a mixed ability group. The course also needs to be stimulating to the participants in order to fire their enthusiasm for the subject and inspire them to learn more about astrology.

For effective learning to take place, any lesson should have a good balance of 'teacher-directed' and 'student-centred' teaching methods. The term 'teacher-directed' describes the imparting of knowledge or information by the teacher to the student, and includes the traditional 'talk and chalk' approach. 'Student-centred' learning shifts the emphasis from the information to the student, developing his or her own capacities and interests through experience. In her book *Theory of Education* Margaret Sutherland describes the term clearly and it applies as much to students in adult education centres as it does to children in schools:

> Possibly one of the major effects of child-centred theory of education is the change it introduces in concepts of the teacher's role. Traditionally the teacher has been seen as the expert possessing knowledge which is

passed on to the child. Now it is proposed that the teacher should retire into the background, simply supplying resources the child may need in the process of discovery learning and in following natural interests in learning. From the creative role of 'moulding the clay' into desired forms, the teacher moves into the apparently less creative role of the gardener. The teacher becomes a 'resource' person, possibly joining with the learner in a co-operative exploration of materials and situation on an equal footing.

These child-centred theories were first introduced by Jean-Jacques Rousseau in *Emile* published in 1762. They were later developed by Maria Montessori, Froebel and A. S. Neill and have been part of our school education for many years. However, only recently have these theories have been applied to adult education and they have many parallels with client-centred therapy.

The renowned American therapist Carl Rogers in his *Freedom to Learn in the 80's* challenges the conventional role of the teacher in a similar fashion and advocates a more 'person-centred' approach to education from nursery schools to universities. The results of his studies showed that with the 'person-centred mode' of education, 'learning tends to be deeper, proceeds at a more rapid rate, and is more pervasive in the life and behaviour of the student.'

Rogers comments that by using a person-centred mode 'We had found a way of being with students that was sharply different from conventional education. It did not involve teaching so much as it involved us in a process that we came to think of as the "facilitation of learning".'

When teaching astrology in adult education, I found it very easy to fall into the expert/authoritative teacher role, often aided by the students' attitude of 'we've come to learn astrology from you'. I was dissatisfied with this kind of teaching situation and wanted to develop a course where learning about astrology was facilitated through the person-centred mode. Through discussions with Prudence Jones and the workshops we led together, I was introduced to 'Creative Astrology' and saw in it the basis for the teaching approach I had been looking for.

I had the opportunity to develop these ideas on Creative Astrology in 1985 when asked to teach a short summer course at the local adult education centre. This five-week course was ideally suited to be one on Creative Astrology for both beginner and experienced students, and its results would be a good measure of how effective this teaching method was. Astrology is a system which seeks to define and describe the world about us, and as adults we already have a deep and personal experience of this world. It was my aim during the course to draw this knowledge and experience from the participants and help them define it in astrological terms. The creative approach would ensure that this process was based on the participants' experience rather than on facts and figures, and would encourage their awareness and understanding of themselves through astrology.

Person-centred education involves 'experience' and 'discovery' methods of teaching. Learning is founded on real experience and observations, and not limited to the verbal level. By using the 'discovery' method, students are given the opportunity to experiment with materials to discover what happens in various situations. With a Creative Astrology course I would have to devise exercises which would enable the students to 'discover' how astrology worked.

In the teaching environment of an adult education course, Creative Astrology needs to have more direction from the tutor, than in the workshop or therapeutic situation. As tutor I would have to provide the resources for learning, and direct the sessions. However, I wanted the emphasis to be on participation and learning through experience. Therefore I aimed to include certain essential criteria when devising the course:

- Tutor's role as guide to educational experiences
- Active participation by the students
- Learning predominantly by 'discovery' techniques (Creative Astrology)
- Accent on co-operative group work and creative expression
- Little concern with conventional academic standards.

Here is a report on the course, offered as a source of practical ideas to other astrologers and teachers of astrology.

The astrological principles covered in the course were:
- **The four elements** – Earth, Air, Fire and Water
- **Twelve signs of the zodiac** – Aries, Taurus, Gemini, Cancer, Leo, Virgo, Libra, Scorpio, Sagittarius, Capricorn, Aquarius and Pisces
- **The planets** – Sun, Moon, Mercury, Venus, Mars, Jupiter, Saturn, Uranus, Neptune, Pluto
- **The major aspects** – opposition, square, conjunction and sextile.

Session One

Fifteen people attended the first session and they were a good mixture of beginner and experienced students. After a general introduction by names and Sun sign, and an agreement about the course content and teaching approach, the principle of the four elements – Earth, Air, Fire and Water – was introduced through carefully selected slides. The pictures were of natural scenes with a strong visual impact. They included a ploughed field, a turning windmill, an erupting volcano, and a seascape.

After discussion of the various responses to the slides – do you like this slide? How does it make you feel? Does it remind you of anything? – I split the group into element groups by Sun signs. People worked in pairs and were given five minutes to discover and discuss their similarities and differences. This 'buzz group' approach is a good ice-breaker giving participants an opportunity to talk and make personal contacts within the class.

The pairs came back into their element groups, and were asked to work out a play based on the actions they would take when faced with a road accident. Quite spontaneously the classic qualities of the elements emerged; stability for Earth; communication for Air; action for Fire and emotion for Water. The Water group displayed a lot of emotional care for the accident victim, though a few tended to collapse once the ambulance had arrived and one member even turned to drink! The Earth group soon became very organised, with each member being given a practical role – getting blankets, phoning 999 and so on. There was lots of activity from the Fire group, who also enthusiastically organised 'traffic control' as well. However, the poor victim in the Air group nearly expired during their lengthy animated discussion on how to go about things! The Air signs are renowned for their communication skills and intellectual approach to life.

The next exercise explored the Moon and the four elements. Our Sun sign represents our *modus operandi*, while the Moon represents our instinctual response to the world. The class was divided into groups by their Moon sign element. The role-play this time was to explore their first instinctual reaction to a crisis. The Earth Moons imagined they were part of an airliner hijack. Earth is practical, self-contained and slow-moving. This group's reaction was to remain in their seats and keep their heads down. The Fire Moons couldn't decide what their reactions would be: 'we just couldn't tell till the real situation happened' – An example perhaps of the impulsive and spontaneous action of Fire. All the Air Moons wanted to do was to 'get on the phone', while Water admitted there might be a few tears along with the 'tea and sympathy'.

The group was gaining an insight into the traditional qualities of the four elements through the impact of their own observations and experiences.

Session Two

Carrying on from the first session, the class was asked to sit in a circle. The Water signs went into the centre. Though only four, they seemed to merge into an undulating mass before our very eyes and calm spread over the room. Next, with boisterous activity the Fire group moved in, and their energy seemed to rush upwards threatening to take off the roof! The Earth signs came quietly and without a world all sat down crossed-legged. The Air group couldn't remain either quiet or still, and sought to make eye contact with others in their friendly way.

All the participants remarked on the strength of the atmosphere the various element groups invoked and their comments showed what a powerful experience it had been:

'You could just see how energetic the Fire signs were.'

'What came over to me was how self-contained the Earth signs were.'

Astrologers often hear 'I don't feel anything like my Sun sign.' When people have conflicting elements in their chart either by Ascendant, Moon or sign emphasis, they can identify strongly with a sign or element other than their Sun sign. I devised an experimental exercise to explore this.

One person with a Leo Sun was shy and quiet. She said she didn't feel anything like a sunny, extrovert Leo, though she did love going to the theatre. Before discovering her Ascendant, I asked her to join the different element groups in turn to see what would happen. She said she felt most comfortable with the Water group and all right with the Earth group. Her Ascendant was Pisces and she had a natal Sun–Saturn conjunction. Pisces is a water sign and Saturn rules the Earth sign of Capricorn. The group commented how comfortable she looked in the Water group. When we

54

repeated the exercise for other people, quite a few said they felt as comfortable, if not more so, in their Ascendant element group.

Session Three

The third session was on the planets and a variety of objects were presented as the focus for discussion. The idea of objects to represent or symbolise the planets comes from Cherry Gilchrist's book *Planetary Symbolism in Astrology* and as she points out the collection will be a subjective one, coloured by one's background and understanding.

After inviting the group to offer what they knew of the planets and the gods they were named after, the objects were presented in planet order. The objects I chose were not exotic, but either decorative or household ones – for example a round brass tray for the golden disc of the Sun, a pearly shell to represent the colour of the Moon which also rules the tides, a holiday brochure for Jupiter as this planet is associated with travelling. I explained to the group how the collection was chosen and we discussed this and other members' reactions and comments.

Then in a five-minute 'quickie' we attempted to discover how well this exercise worked for the group. We all emptied our pockets and bags to see what we could make of the articles inside – credit cards symbolised the extravagance of Jupiter, a pocket knife the aggression of Mars, perfume the beauty of Venus while to others it symbolised the allure of Neptune!

To end this session there was a short guided visualisation. My aim was to explore through this technique any strong connections people might have with a particular planet and how this could be related to their birth chart. What happened was very interesting as some individuals visualised a planet which was strong by transit at the time of the exercise.

55

Guided Visualisation

> Sit comfortably on the chair with your feet on the ground. Become aware of your spine and gradually allow it to become straight. Observe the rise and fall of your breath, how it comes in and out. Begin to imagine you're somewhere in the country. Feel the fresh air on your cheeks, hear the birds singing and smell the summer flowers. Look down to your feet, they are on a path – what kind of path is it? Is it broad or narrow? Soft and sandy or full of stones? Once you can see your path and feel the earth under your feet, begin to follow the path, observing where it takes you. On and on you walk – do you find it a pleasant experience or are you getting tired? As you look up you notice a figure coming towards you. What does this figure look like? How is it dressed? Is it a man or a woman? You notice the figure is holding something in his/her hand. He/she has a gift for you – take it. Feel its weight in your hand, look at it and see what it is. The figure is now moving away, bid him/her farewell and begin your journey back along the path. Choose what you wish to do with your gift – put it in your pocket, hide it under a stone perhaps. Now you have reached the end of the path, so get ready to return to this room. Feel the floor under your feet, your body on the chair, become aware of the people on either side of you and the sound of my voice. Gradually in your own time, open your eyes and be with the group again.

Guided visualisations are best taken slowly, with plenty of time for everyone to proceed at their own rate. The sharing session need not be to the whole group as experiences from visualisation can be very personal. Group members were invited to share their visualisation with the person sitting next to them. In this situation there are usually enough members to share and very often some who are happy to share to the whole group.

Here are the experiences of two women both with a Sun conjunction to another planet – one by transit and the other natally:

(1) My path was through a wood with dappled sunlight shining through the trees. It led to a clearing with a deep valley and mountains on the opposite side. I could see a river winding through the bottom of the valley. Coming towards me was a man riding on a white horse. He looked like a king with a gold circlet on his head and a purple cloak. He gave me a wooden box and when I opened it, there was frankincense inside.

Jupiter is associated with the power of emperors and kings, as well as wide open spaces and horses! Traditionally its colour is purple. This woman was asked if she had a strong Jupiter in her chart. She explained that she had Sun conjunct Mercury in Gemini natally, and that at present Jupiter was transiting her Sun. Like the transit, her figure representing Jupiter was not static, but travelling through her visualisation on a horse. She added she had a deep affinity with frankincense, which she associated with kings.

(2) I was following a mountain path on the edge of a deep ravine. No one came to meet me, but I was aware of a figure following me. It was an old man with a long grey beard and long dark robes. He was bent over a staff and reminded me of the pictures you see of Old Father Time. He wasn't threatening and I didn't feel frightened as it was like having a guardian angel following me. He didn't give me a gift as such, just a feeling of security and safety because he was there.

Saturn as Cronus is the god of time and is often depicted as an old man with a sickle. Saturn is the planet of responsibility, duty and tradition and is associated with dark colours and winter. This woman has a Sun–Saturn conjunction in Cancer in her 1st house.

Her Sun is in front of Saturn, and so in her visualisation this planet followed her, symbolising her natal aspect. Cancer is a sign renowned for needing security, and as a group we felt that some of the qualities (structure, discipline) of Saturn provided her with that security.

It is interesting to note that the natal aspect to the Sun was visualised as a permanent feature, while the transit aspect was symbolised as a travelling figure passing through.

Session Four

This time the group brought their objects to symbolise the planets. They included some fascinating and amusing collections. One woman brought different coloured and sized marbles she had taken from her son's collection. She related her choice to the traditional colours for the planets – silver for Mercury, pink for Venus, red for Mars, while another woman brought all pieces of jewellery – gold ring for the Sun, pearls for the Moon, a piece of jet for Saturn, a pair of Titanium earrings for Uranus. One very inventive collection was totally based on food and drink from the kitchen. What stands out vividly in my mind was the black pudding for the 'blood and guts' of Mars, yeast to represent the awakening aspect of Uranus, and wine for the escapism of Neptune. There was an orange for the Sun, cheese for the Moon and bread for Jupiter because the flour expanded during its preparation and too much could be fattening! Though this was a light-hearted approach, it displayed the interest and participation of the group.

During this session the planetary aspects were explored. Four props were presented to the group – a crown, a large-brimmed black hat, an army officer's hat and a lace shawl. The groups split into Mercury sign groups and selected a prop to experiment with. However, before we got that far, one woman grabbed the shawl, flung it round her shoulders and put on the hat.

'How typical of a Scorpio!' came the comment from another person. Scorpios tend to get what they want, and they love dressing in black. The woman in question was a Gemini with Scorpio rising and she certainly looked wonderful in the two items. A man commented he had often noticed how Geminis seem to like wearing scarves. Everyone agreed that the whole ensemble was very typical of Scorpio's way of dressing.

There were two very different reactions to the army hat. One woman seized it joyfully, stuck it on her head at a jaunty angle, pushing her hair up underneath, and took on a flirtatious role. A man in the same group expressed a real aversion to the hat and its military connections.

When we turned to their birth charts, the woman had a Mars–Venus conjunction and the man a Mars–Saturn square. As the goddess of love, Venus would soften Mars' aggression when these two planets are in aspect. The two planets have a mutual attraction as in Roman mythology they were lovers. Saturn, however, with its limitation and caution, inhibits the natural drive of Mars. Mars is the god of war, and this group interpreted the soldier's hat as having martial symbolism. From this example the group could see how a planet's action is modified by its aspects.

The idea of aspects being a relationship or communication between planets was explored in the following exercise.

Working in pairs, the class began a conversation on an astrological topic. Then they had to explore the effect on their conversation when they:

- sat opposite each other
- sat back to back
- sat side by side
- walk towards each other from opposite sides of the room
- stood at a point in the room where they had no eye contact with their partner.

59

Obviously it's much harder to communicate with a partner when there is no eye contact or seen body language to convey subtle messages. A friendly stance while talking with a partner – either facing or side by side – was experienced as supportive and conducive to communication. These exercises were likened to a conjunction aspect with compatible and incompatible planets and the following examples suggested:

> Side by side could represent Venus and the Moon as these planets are similar; while facing each other could be Uranus and Mercury, as it's a good position to exchange ideas. But those two probably wouldn't remain seated for long! The back to back position might represent a Saturn–Mars conjunction as they have such opposite actions.

Gradually the group began to get the feel of what astrological aspects might represent to the planets involved. The pairs joined into fours to share their observations and experiences.

Session Five

As a revision of the last session a very short guided visualisation was used. This one took the form of entering a junk shop and finding a mirror with a very special frame. Participants were asked to sketch their mirrors and then invited to share their drawings with the rest of the group. In devising this exercise I took the mirror to represent the Moon, with its reflective quality and round shape. By introducing a frame, I hoped this might represent another planet in aspect with the Moon.

A Moon trine Neptune woman found an oval mirror with a frame of real seashells. When she looked into the mirror, she saw a mermaid sitting on a rock in the middle of the sea. The Moon rules women, while Neptune rules the sea and all its creatures. In this person's visualisation, the traditional symbols of the planets were very strong.

Another person described their experience as follows: 'I found a round mirror with an ornate frame of flowers and scrolls. In it I saw a room with an open window. It looked like my room, but no one was at home!'

This person has a Moon trine Pluto aspect. The Moon also rules Cancer, the sign of the home. As she has Cancer on the Ascendant, not surprisingly she saw her home in the mirror. Our group wasn't sure about the Pluto aspect – some people thought as Pluto is the god of riches, the ornate frame represented this. Others commented that as no one was at home, Pluto could be an unseen force in her home! As Pluto is also the god of the underworld, someone suggested the open window could be an entrance to his domain.

It has been my own experience when both learning and teaching astrology that the aspects were the most difficult principle to grasp fully. Personally I often experience and observe the aspects through physical sensation and body movement and I wanted to find a more non-verbal, physical example to offer the group.

The group had observed how a planet's aspects might modify its expression, and to facilitate learning about the different nature of each aspect, we tried the 'rope' exercise. In astrology we learn about the conflict of the T-square and the harmony of a trine. I hoped to show this strain and ease through the using ropes to represent the aspects.

The group sat in a circle defining the 360° of the chart. Two members opposite each other were asked to stand and hold a rope between them. They explored ways of holding and pulling the rope, from a tug-of-war to equilibrium. The opposition was in action before our very eyes. A third member joined the pair at their midpoint, looping his rope round the first at half way to form a T-square. Number three then pulled, one and two pulled back and a state of conflict and imbalance was observed.

The trine was expressed by using the Grand Trine as an

example with three people at equidistant points in the circle. The lack of tension in the ropes was clearly seen in comparison to the previous exercise. Those involved in the exercise commented how comfortable and happy they felt in this stance. Everyone in the class had the opportunity to experience the different feel of the ropes for the opposition, T-square and trine. They commented how clearly they felt the friction of the T-square and the easy, laid-back quality of the Grand Trine.

The idea of the tension and strength of a Grand Cross is often difficult to grasp, but this example was most success-ful when illustrated by the ropes. From the imbalance of the T-square, the second rope was unlooped and one end passed over to a fourth person. The tension was great on the ropes as all four individuals pulled together, and yet they were equally poised. A member commented: 'The Grand Cross is like a com-plete entity. Its pattern seems to dominate the whole room.'

The nature of the planets involved was then introduced through role play. The first pair acted 'Jupiter opposite Saturn' using the ropes, and their conversation ran something like this:

Jupiter: – Hello I'm Jupiter. Isn't it a great day? Let's do something really exciting. I know – we can bunk off work and go horse-riding. Then we can take in a spot of lunch at 'Mario's'. He has some brilliant wines we could try!
Saturn: – Don't be so irresponsible, you know we've got the auditors coming in this week, so there's masses of work to do. Anyway I never drink at lunchtime, it's bad for the digestion!
Jupiter: You're always such a spoil-sport.
Saturn: I don't mean to be, but you know I'm scared of horses.

At this point the two were stopped and a solution or balance for this conflict invited. Someone suggested that if Jupiter helped Saturn with the work, they might have time to go riding afterwards. Another member commented that as Jupiter had no eye for detail this could cause more work for

Saturn checking up on him. A third member retorted that Mars was the careless one always in a rush. I listened with pleasure – astrology had begun to pervade their experience and they were able to discuss its principles with understanding.

At a suggestion from the group, we tried to create a birth chart using people and ropes for the planets and aspects. Armed with a volunteer plus his chart, the zodiac was marked out by a circle of twelve chairs each representing a sign. We made sure the Ascendant rose in the east and placed the volunteer outside the circle. Ten members elected to be the planets and each with their planetary label took up their positions holding the ropes – quite a difficult management feat! The volunteer moved around the circle from the Ascendant to IC, then to the Descendant and Midheaven – the four sensitive points of the chart.

The volunteer, who already had some knowledge of his chart, commented on how this exercise enabled him to be more objective about his chart, and to realise he had choices about his attitude to certain planets – there was always a different point of view!

This living representation of the birth chart was a very fitting exercise to draw the session and course to an end. As they left, one woman commented: 'I'll never forget the ropes. It made the aspects really clear. You can see the tension in the opposition, and the instability of the T-square.'

This exercise has been used again with other groups, and it offers individuals the opportunity to contact the dynamics within their own personalities through directing a role–play with the planets. When dealing with this kind of very personal role–play, it is wise to have a tutor/facilitator with some expertise in psychodrama.

In subsequent courses of ten and twenty weeks for both beginners and intermediate students, a large portion of the course was devoted to Creative Astrology. As group feeling becomes stronger with a longer course, group members have time to become more familiar and comfortable with this approach. During the initial course some were reticent

63

in the role-playing and sharing sessions. But it was always up to them whether they were participants or passive observers. As I come to know a group better, situations and exercises can be devised to suit particular interests and creative expression – drama, art work or movement.

With a group experienced in both astrology and group work, we were having difficulty, not surprisingly, in verbalising Pluto transits! The transits of Pluto can represent a time of deep and transformative changes within us, which can be uncomfortable and even painful. Using lumps of clay we allowed our fingers to mould shapes that expressed our feelings about these transformative transits – dragons, spirals, gods, goddesses, and abstract shapes emerged from the clay. In the following sharing session we discovered that externalising feelings into a form gave a focus for discussion and an opportunity to gain insight into our experiences of Pluto.

In a workshop based on the planets, led by Lynn Bagnall, a Surrey circle dance teacher and myself, the participants experienced Venus through dance. Mike O'Neill's computer studies show that Venus has a celestial ballet to a five/eight rhythm. Its orbit initially makes a heart shape (in 412 days) and progresses on to form a five-petal or rose shape after exactly eight years. The heart and the rose are traditional symbols of Venus. Five dancers formed a circle, and one by one they danced the heart shape. Each person danced the circle, coming in to form the loop and then out again. When nearest the earth (inferior conjunction), Venus always presents the same face. The dancers faced the centre of the circle, which represented the earth, each time they looped into the centre. To make the ballet flow, each dancer moved onto the next person's position, once they had completed their circle. This was repeated five times. Then the dancers moved simultaneously five times. Before our very eyes the rose shape opened and closed. Abstract, astronomical data had come alive through dance, and the beauty of Venus was there for everyone to experience.

64

VENUS OVER
412 DAYS
THE HEART

VENUS OVER
2922 DAYS
THE ROSE

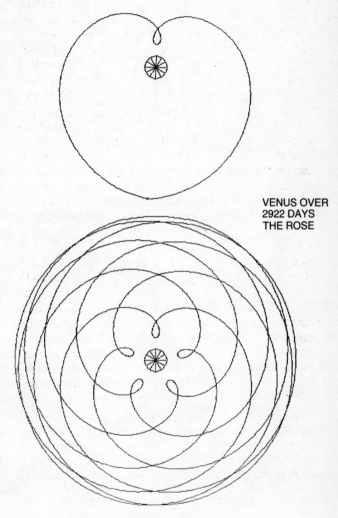

Fig. 3   The Dance of Venus

Conclusions

By using a creative technique to teach astrology in adult education, I found that it promotes an opportunity for people to learn about astrology in their own way and through their own experiences of the world. And as the examples of this course show, Creative Astrology is an effective way to learn. It promotes a deeper understanding of astrological principles in a shorter time than a solely 'information imparting' method. Creative Astrology is a technique which can be used successfully with groups of mixed experience and knowledge of astrology, and enables the tutor to join with the students in a co-operative exploration of astrology.

> I hear and I do
> I see and I know
> I do and I understand
>
> Ancient Chinese Poem

Note: With grateful thanks to all members of the 1985 group, in particular June Abraham and Louise Wren, for their participation, observations and comments. Also thanks to Nick Kollerstrom for telling me about Mike O'Neill's work, and Lynn Bagnall for her contribution to the Venus dance.

Bibliography

Froebel, F., tr. S.S.F. Fletcher & J. Welton, *Froebel's Chief Writings on Education Rendered into English*, Educational Classics, London, 1912

Gilchrist, Cherry, *Planetary Symbolism in Astrology*, Astrological Association/Saros Foundation, London, 1980

Montessori, Maria, tr. H.W. Holmes, *The Montessori Method*, Heinemann, London, 1912

Neill, A.S., *Summerhill, a Radical Approach to Education*, Gollancz, London, 1962

Rogers, Carl, *Freedom to Learn in the 1980s*, Charles Merrill, N.Y., 1983

Rousseau, J.J., tr. B. Foxley, *Emile*, Everyman, London, 1974

Sutherland, M., *The Theory of Education*, Longman, London, 1988

4

ASTROLOGICAL PSYCHOTHERAPY

Jochen and Ulrike Encke

Commentary

With the next essay we return to psychotherapy, and specifically to the unconscious dynamics of the group. Jochen and Ulrike Encke describe their method of 'playing the horoscope': allowing it to express its dynamics quite spontaneously through the real-life situations of participants in any given workshop. By simply accepting that the workshop will express the nature of the horoscope under scrutiny, the Enckes find that somehow it actually does. This approach is a deliberate invocation of the 'synchronicity' which may spontaneously occur in more conventional therapeutic situations. The authors' theoretical analysis of why such deliberate invocation can and should be possible makes illuminating reading. They are also at pains to point out the necessity of drawing clear boundaries, of containing such an expansive, 'centrifugal' approach and balancing it with the practical, 'centripetal' outlook of responsible adult life. As the earlier contributors have already hinted, astrology offers a framework which not only invites but actually demands that we balance what is within with what is without, what is spontaneous with what is controlled, what is individual with what is collective. Here we see this principle unmistakably in action.

P. H. J.

What is the history of what we call 'ASTROLOGICAL PSY-CHOTHERAPY'? How did we develop it? To answer this, we have to say something about our personal life-stories, since the work we are doing is not something we decided to do, planned and then put into action. Rather, it is something which has developed over the past five years. However, the first seeds were sown much earlier.

I, Jochen, remember my first visit to an astrologer defini-tively as one of the important stepping stones. In the late 1970s I was studying psychology and sociology at the University of Münster, West Germany. I had also started a training in humanistic psychotherapy, when owing to some strange circumstances I found myself with an appointment for an astrological consultation. Astrology was – and still is – quite unacceptable to the scientifically-oriented outlook of a university. I think that I went partly to prove that 'star-gazing' was nonsense. However, the experience astonished me. How surprised I was about all the details the astrologer could reveal by looking at my birth chart, how much he could say about my psychological background, my parents, my dreams, hopes and fantasies. It was very interesting and helpful to discover meaning in my past and present crisis, and to witness my life being unfolded in front of me. But what really threw me and what changed my outlook on reality and my life profoundly were not these facts, not this additional information about myself. What threw me was not so much *what* he had to say about me but the very fact that he could talk about my life so meaningfully without knowing me. An entire new world opened its doors to me, a world which was so different to the world I had encountered so far. Just the fact that the astrologer, by looking at my horoscope, was able to describe my parents so clearly and distinctly had very deep implications for my studies. However, astrology and my interest in it remained a well-kept secret for a while: it would have been unthinkable, within the framework of a scientific understanding of human development, to suggest for instance that, since one's parents can be found so clearly in one's own horoscope, the individual might have 'chosen' his/her parents, thus being entirely responsible for what he/she has become. The basic assumption of astrology, that of the oneness and interconnectedness of all, 'as above so below', its search for meaning and purpose, rather than for causes, left a deep impression on me right from the beginning. Some ten years later, Ulrike and I, having 'joined forces', gradually found a way not only to make use of astrological concepts and insights for psychotherapeutic work, but actually to combine astrology and psychotherapy and experience them as complementary to each other.

I, Ulrike, cannot lay claim to any magical peak experience that brought me to astrology and led me to our approach. It feels surprisingly clear, on looking back, how every event I experienced, all the kicks and blows in my life, have been stepping stones for my work today, and blessings in disguise if I was able to utilise them. I became involved with astrology because I was dissatisfied with my life, and the traditional answers to my questions concerning the meaning of life did not satisfy me at all. I had a friend who had recently started to study astrology; I was amused by his fascination with the whole subject. One evening he showed me his astrology cards and explained them to me. One could ask questions and they would be answered with 'yes', 'no', and 'there is a conflict', which itself was explained by the symbols of the cards. We played with quite trivial issues. None the less I became interested, copied his set of cards and by doing so learned the symbols, and started laying cards for anyone who asked me to. Strangely enough I could say something every time and it even made sense. Some people were quite surprised and felt they had been helped. Gradually I stopped laughing and took it more seriously.

I started reading astrology books, at the same time learning through being in psychotherapy. Gradually I was able to make more sense of my life and of the many times I had felt lost, different from everybody else. I had not been able to reason or explain any of my decisions or actions. Friends used to say I was like a feather: just a little breeze and off I went. Yet I remember distinctly being only eight years old, and thinking that my life was all mapped out for me, that I was on a path – although I could not see around the next corner. There was a strange sense of security going with it and it took away some of the pain and awkwardness I had so often felt. Astrological thinking therefore felt quite natural to me, and it was not long before I had found a way to incorporate it into my work.

We started working professionally in the field of psychotherapy and astrology, but they were still kept separate: we were running psychotherapy groups and astrology classes; we offered individual psychotherapy and astrological horoscope interpretations. Clients came to us either for psychotherapy or astrology. In 1984 we started working together. The astrology classes were becoming more emotional; we started experiencing astrological symbols rather than just understanding them intellectually. Our work grew with each workshop, but it took another year or so until we suddenly realised that in our workshops we had started literally applying and experiencing the basic philosophy of astrology: that of holism, the oneness of all. The Buddhistic saying, 'All is in one, and the one is in all', was not just an intellectual concept anymore. We not only taught the idea of 'synchronicity', of 'as above so below', but tried to give students an opportunity to experience it for themselves. Then, after having done a series of three workshops with the same group, we realised that we had found a way of successfully combining astrology and psychotherapy.

Before we start describing our approach in detail we would like to talk about some ideas and concepts first. The knowledge that everything is interconnected and has one and the same centre opens a vast field of psychotherapeutic opportunities. Whatever is happening in the outer world can be used as a symbol, which is then seen as coinciding with the inner life experiences. Understanding the symbol can give a profound insight into oneself.

In recent years the existence of an inner psychic world as a reality besides our outer physical world has been increasingly accepted. At least since Freud the importance of dreams and the existence an unconscious which can 'interfere' with reality has been widely acknowledged. Jung then introduced into psychology the idea of an interplay between inner and outer worlds, the possibility of using outer events as meaningful symbols rather than just seeing the outer world as being affected by a distressed psyche. The discovery of the collective unconscious by Jung, and of the acausal ordering of the subatomic world by modern physics, has pushed us beyond a merely rational and causal interpretation of reality, making us aware that on some level there is no separation, only oneness.

An example from our psychotherapeutic practice may illustrate how a symbol can be used. A client, whom we will call Rod, was sharing his thoughts about terminating therapy. As we discussed the pros and cons, suddenly the table lamp next to him went out. I stood up to switch it on again, jokingly saying that the lamp might be communicating something to him. The following session Rod stated surprisingly clearly that he would like to continue therapy, since he felt there was something there waiting to be discovered. We did not go further into what it might be until about two months later. While he was sharing a dream with me I suddenly started thinking about the incident with the lamp and I asked him whether it had made a much greater impact on him, and maybe even on the decision to continue therapy, than he dared to acknowledge. At that very moment the lamp went out again: we were left sitting in a nearly dark room. One could have heard a needle drop – the atmosphere was so charged. Rod was quite a rationalist, down-to-earth person, and he obviously felt rather embarrassed as he confessed how deeply he had felt moved by that experience two months ago and that it really had made him change his mind and had helped him to decide to continue

71

coming. Then suddenly the lamp went on again.

This event goes beyond a rational interpretation of our everyday physical reality. We cannot assume that Rod's power, coupled with mine, had caused the lamp to go out. Nor can we reduce the experience solely to the fact that a wire was not properly connected. This would not take into account the fact that the lamp's behaviour was coinciding meaningfully with several very significant moments in the encounter between Rod and myself. Once we start to take the lamp's behaviour as a symbol assuming it is interconnected with Rod's life, then we can use this event creatively to clarify and deepen the understanding of his personal life. The lamp and Rod's life are two different principles, not normally connected. In the experience they unite and are seen as interconnected. These acausal events in which two incommensurable facts coincide are called, in Jungian language, 'synchronistic events'. Sychronistic events take place since what we perceive as separate has only been separated artificially by our rational mind. But actually the universe is not separate from man, the group is not separate from the individual, each individual is not separate from the other, inside is not separate from outside.

To clarify this, let us look for a moment at our logo, a double mandala, which we found in M.-L. von Franz' book *On Divination and Synchronicity* (see Figure 4). This double mandala shows two identical wheels intercepting each other. From the viewpoint of our everyday physical world, with its

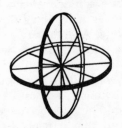

Fig.4 Double mandala

72

rational and causal outlook on reality, the two wheels would destroy each other if they started rotating – unless we gave them each a separate identity, with its own separate axis.

From the viewpoint of what we call the psychic world reality, the impossible becomes possible: we can imagine the two wheels spinning around their common axis without destroying each other. The psychic world is not restricted by time or space. In dreams for instance we can fly, but we are bound by the law of gravity when awake. Boundaries do not exist in the psychic world. Its reality is four-dimensional, and therefore timeless, obeying an eternal order. From this point of view we can look at one principle (for example Rod and his individual life circumstances) and know that it is not separate from the other principles (the lamp's behaviour). Actually they are identical, having one and the same root, the same identity, and are happening synchronously.

The framework within which we interpret these experiences of synchronicity needs to be very well defined, lest they lead to a narcissistic outlook on the world in which everything is seen as a reflection or extension of oneself, or even to a kind of insanity in which everything is seen as a message, in which one feels possessed by one's inner life. At the end we all belong to the realm of the physical world, in which we are separate beings in charge of the surrounding world and of our fate.

How synchronicity is brought into the circle, how oneness and interconnectedness are experienced in a group setting, will be illustrated by the following extract from a workshop.

In order to describe a workshop we need to select, exclude, separate – and this is exactly what the experiences in our workshops are not about. It is a bit like listening to an orchestra while it is playing and trying to sort out the notes coming from a single instrument. It is an almost impossible task. Intellectually we cannot grasp 'oneness', but we can allow ourselves to be grasped by the experience of it. Hopefully we will be able to communicate some of our experience.

A woman, whom we will call Sue, and whose horoscope is shown in Figure 5 (we have changed all names and withheld birth data for reasons of confidentiality) wants her horoscope to be worked on in the group. The time allowed for this is one hour. She sits outside the group circle, does not participate in the activities of the group, and is asked only to observe what is happening in the group. Her horoscope is drawn in the middle of the group and each participant receives the astrological symbol he or she is sitting closest to.

For reasons of space we will have to simplify our explanation of the way in which we work, and because of that we cannot possibly do justice to the complexity of emotions and the dynamics of the group. Moreover we are only able to focus on a very small section of the horoscope. The reader must keep in mind that this allows only a distorted view of the horoscope, since any astrological work needs to take into account the whole horoscope, its whole energy and – in our case – the dynamics of the whole group.

At the time of the workshop Neptune in Sue's horoscope (see Figure 5) is transited by Pluto, hence the whole aspect configuration – Moon conjunct Neptune in Scorpio in the 11th square Saturn in Capricorn conjunct Jupiter in Aquarius in the 2nd – is under a specific tension. Nicole receives Neptune in Scorpio in the 11th, Sabina Saturn in Capricorn in the 2nd, and Petra is transiting Pluto, therefore sitting directly behind Nicole/Neptune. (As Neptune is conjunct the Moon, and Saturn is conjunct Jupiter, we ought to keep the importance of these symbols in mind as well.)

We trust that each planet describes accurately the individual group member at this specific moment in time. We agree that during the course of the workshop, especially during the time we have agreed to work on the horoscope, whatever is said, whatever is happening in the group will be accepted as meaningful – not only for the group members sitting in the circle, but also for Sue, whose inner dynamics will be seen as identical with those of the group. Each group member, whatever she is doing or feeling or thinking, will be seen as a significant and meaningful symbol for all the other members and for Sue. We decide to forget the horoscope and

74

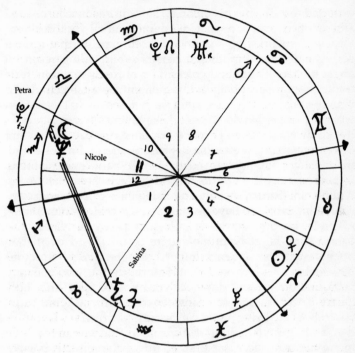

Fig. 5 Sue

Sue and ask each group member to be truly him/herself,
without thinking about the horoscope, specifically the planet
they represent.

Nicole, or Neptune, is a rather small woman, with something of the fairy in her appearance. She feels very ambivalent
in the group; indeed she has hardly participated. She has
a nap during the lunch break and does not really feel like
playing. We suggest that she can be as she is, and does
not need to play; she has already become Neptune without
realising it, even without being able to avoid it. She works
in the art world, buying and selling paintings; however, she is
not clear about why she does it, as she does not enjoy it at all.
Her mother died very early and as the oldest daughter she was

expected to look after her siblings. She still needs to be needed and sacrifices a lot of herself in order to maintain this position. During the workshop she finds herself experiencing quite a strong need to be mothered herself – and rather resentful about the fact that nobody picks it up or reacts to it. She feels under pressure especially at this moment, because Petra/Pluto is sitting behind her, she cannot see her and – what feels even worse – Petra either does not feel like saying anything, or does not know what to say. Nicole experiences the pressure as not directly related to Petra/Pluto, being triggered by her sitting behind her, but not caused by her. What Nicole/Neptune is bothered with and thinking of a lot is her relationship with Sabina/Saturn. Nicole and Sabina are close friends, but something seems to have become stuck in their relationship.

Before looking at the relationship between Nicole and Sabina (that is, at Neptune square Saturn), and what they might symbolise to each other, we first try to find out how Sabina is feeling (what Saturn in the 2nd means). Sabina/Saturn shares how unworthy she feels and how insecure she is. She is a single parent with a young boy. She has been living on social security, which embarrasses her, and she often finds it difficult to find enough money to maintain an acceptable standard of living. The present difficulties with Nicole affect her strongly and do not help her at all to feel at ease in the group. Not having been able to pay the whole fee for the workshop seems an additional burden. (Nicole had given her part of the fee!) Now we know quite a lot more about who Nicole/Neptune and Sabina/Saturn in the 2nd, are. The next step will be to explore what the square between Neptune (conjunct Moon) in the 11th and Saturn (and Jupiter) in the 2nd means for each of them. This square, although manifesting itself in the tension between Nicole and Sabina, must ultimately be seen as an inner dynamic within each of them.

Sabina now starts sharing what is so clearly symbolised by Nicole's Neptune in the 11th conjunct the Moon: her confusion about who she is as a woman. The struggle to keep her son's and her own life together seems to leave hardly any space for herself, to discover who she is and what she wants to do, and it isolates her from her friends. Sabina has no Water in her horoscope and a lot of Fire. However, she learned very early on in life that her active, outgoing and creative side was not very well perceived. Therefore she had in a way trained herself to be what she thought a woman was expected to be: housebound and dedicated to looking after others. She created for herself a mask of sentimentality, weepiness and vulnerability in order to find acceptance. When she talks she often experiences herself as being so draining, confused and dishonest that hardly anybody cares really to listen. For her, being a housebound single mother feeds into this pattern of not being able to use her Fire in the way she wants. But it may also be seen – as she discovers – as an excuse for not daring to rediscover who she really is.

Nicole/Neptune in turn now starts sharing – as we will later on find out is so accurately described by Sabina's Saturn in the 2nd conjunct Jupiter – that her entire life got turned upside down because of the recent bank crash in which she lost most of her money. She feels ashamed to acknowledge how wealthy she actually was and still is. But even more she finds it difficult to accept the fact that money has been ruling her life and that her striving for more wealth and security has isolated and imprisoned her. She discovers how she tends to 'buy' people. When she spends money for and on other people she feels needed. However, feeling needed, having a social and active life does not give her a sense of inner strength and wealth – on the contrary: she feels how dependent she herself actually is on others.

Sabina realises that on the one hand she is grateful to Nicole for having paid part of the workshop fees, but on the other hand she sees how Nicole's need to be needed is feeding the helpless side, where she feels so unworthy and out of contact with her true being. She discovers how important it is to take an active step out of her isolation and suffering. Joining a women's group (Neptune in the 11th), something she wanted to do for a long time but kept on postponing, would be one of those steps.

For Nicole it is quite a revelation to see something positive in the loss of money (Saturn and Jupiter in the 2nd). She has become aware that the material world cannot provide her with the security, stability and friendship she missed so much as a child. But more important than that: Nicole starts resenting her role as 'mother' and acknowledges the urge to have Sabina as a woman friend rather than a replacement of her siblings whom she can look after. In the struggle to become more authentic they have both trapped each other by reacting to the other's neurotic pattern rather than helping the other person to grow beyond them. Instead of confronting the issues within themselves they started making the relationship responsible for the frustration and anger of not being able to separate from the past.

We are dealing here with very personal and often very early feelings and experiences which ought to be treated with respect and never be seen as less important than the excitement about synchronistic events or about a technique. During the work we do not forget – as we have done in this article for the purpose of clarity – the actual owner of the horoscope. If his or her feelings cannot be contained until the end of the exploration, they can be shared at any point in the proceedings. Obviously the horoscope owner is very deeply involved since all that is happening in the group is a reflection of her own life-story.

Sue's mother was blind when she was born. Sue felt guilty about it all her life, as if she had caused her suffering, or as if there was something wrong in being able to see. Sue still lives with her mother and sees no possibility of ever leaving this helpless woman and starting to lead her own life. Witnessing Sabina sharing her feelings about her femininity helped her to acknowledge her own confusion. For Sue this indicates that new doors have been opened in her own life. The bank crash she sees as the sudden loss of her mother's financial support that will ensue if she decides to leave home. Never before has

78

she been able to experience so clearly as by witnessing the group, how stuck she had felt all her life. She describes the stuckness as being torn between the fear of losing her mother – the financial security provided by her mother if she leaves on the one hand (Saturn and Jupiter in the 2nd) – and on the other hand the inability to develop her own womanhood and to feel free and independent (Neptune conjunct the Moon in the 11th) if she stays. She discovers that money might have been a way for her mother to avoid her own feelings and to buy her daughter's support. Sue also sees how much she herself is dependent on being needed by her mother in order to feel worth something. Instead of blaming her mother and making her and her suffering responsible for her difficulties in leading her own life, Sue needs to take an active step away from her mother. By doing so she will discover that maybe her mother is not so helpless after all (as Sabina is not). Sue can survive without financial support – she might even enjoy standing on her own feet – and both are able to cope with the fear of separation they did not want to confront within themselves.

Sabina and Nicole are now able to understand quite a bit more about each other and about themselves. They feel much warmer towards each other. As they represent part of Sue's psyche something has changed within Sue.

Some time after the workshop we heard that Sue had left home, refusing to take any money, although it had been offered to her. After a stressful time her relationship with her mother (specifically her attitude towards her own womanhood) had very much improved, to Sue's satisfaction. We believe that this is only one reflection of a deep emotional change, which was not caused by the group, but coincided with what was happening in the group and was therefore only made conscious by the group.

It is quite a magical experience to discover that before trying to play a specific planet one already is the planet; before actually starting to think about the horoscope, the group has already become the horoscope. The individual group member and the planet, the group and the horoscope, although

79

separate principles, suddenly unite and are experienced as one and the same. The planet one receives at random and 'plays' is always very appropriate and full of meaning. The person who represents for example, Saturn, always plays a Saturnian role in the group. But more than that: the Saturnian role coincides with Saturnian thoughts or feelings one is being confronted with at the present moment. In one workshop for instance a woman found herself contemplating her role in the group. She felt outside of the group, because she had organised the workshop and felt responsible for it. When she was given the role of Saturn to play, she suddenly realised, and was able to discuss, the extent to which the burden of responsibility had been with her throughout almost her entire life, and also how lost she felt if she could not define her role as that of 'the organiser'. Looking at the angular relationship of Saturn in the presented horoscope and working with the dynamics of the group members who are at the other sides of the aspects to Saturn will help her to understand more clearly what she is doing and why, and will help her to find her way back to the group and to a more authentic way of dealing with others in her life.

At the end of another workshop we once 'played' one aspect of a group member's horoscope: a Moon–Pluto opposition. The group members already felt very tired and overloaded but we had agreed to do this one aspect before ending. As we laid the horoscope in the middle of the group the two people who were sitting nearest to the symbols had already done a lot of work during the course of the workshop and did not want to do any more as they felt exhausted. Nicole, representing the Moon, gave in easily. But Sharon, representing Pluto, protested strongly, even moved her chair back to indicate that she did not want to have anything to do with the interaction. The more Nicole and the group tried to persuade Sharon to join in, the more Sharon withdrew even further – and it seemed the more Sharon withdrew the more Nicole became involved, trying to manipulate Sharon, feeling rejected and hurt. By that time the group was enveloped in an atmosphere of heavy silence. Only just before we decided to stop the 'play' did both Nicole and Sharon admit how much rage they felt behind the withdrawal, tiredness and hurt – and how much fear of the rage, which could have become violent at any minute, they experienced.

The owner of the horoscope was intrigued by how familiar the atmosphere in the room felt to her. Not only did she know about Nicole's role, which she mainly played in the relationship with her mother (she was the fifth child and her mother had not really wanted her), but also Sharon's. For once, she was able to observe from the outside what she usually experienced as a dynamic between her and others and as an inner struggle. As an observer she was able to see how Nicole and Sharon provoked each other and the rage and fear in each of them. This rage was familiar to her, she usually hid it behind tiredness, helplessness, being hurt, and only expressed it through withdrawing. She was surprised to see how much she habitually deadened herself, and how much energy there actually was in her, but how afraid she was of it. In her life this has often been reflected by the fact that whenever she became too successful, too powerful or too close to somebody, she sabotaged her own position.

We may have an idea or concept about a specific planet and its angular relationship with other planets, we may have an insight into a horoscope, may know how to interpret it, to diagnose the challenges, conflicts and potentials; however, ultimately a horoscope is like a crystal, always changing, always revealing new aspects and new dimensions. To do real justice to the complexity of a planet and that of a horoscope, we have to leave the world of words and thoughts behind us.

If we use the idea of oneness and interconnectedness and put it into practice, then just by observing an individual group member we can learn and understand much more about the planet he or she is representing than any astrology book can teach us. By allowing the group dynamics to unfold and accepting them as a reflection of a specific horoscope or aspects of a horoscope we can become observers of a much clearer mind, a much stronger force than even the most sophisticated interpretation can provide.

In this way psychotherapeutic work enriches astrology, deepens the interpretation of a horoscope and widens the understanding of how a specific individual ticks. Psychotherapy can help to bring a horoscope alive, can bring synchronicity into the circle and help us to *experience* astrological thinking. For psychotherapy the horoscope provides a structural framework which is needed to explore more deeply some of the mysteries of relating and how people interact, how they are interconnected and how everyone has an important and unique position within a group setting or society in general. Astrology can help to open up transpersonal, mystical and religious – in the broadest sense of the word – dimensions in psychotherapeutic work, which can often lead to an entirely new understanding, a new philosophy of one's life.

We believe that there is an innate drive in all of us towards a spiritual and religious understanding of our lives. Although we may love worshipping our own will and power, there is a deep yearning for something greater than ourselves. To accept this yearning as part of our nature is essential – especially in our present times – for a creative and fulfilling life. As the interplay between two different forces, the centripetal and centrifugal force, keeps our solar system in balance, so is the interplay between rational everyday reality and the mystical world reality essential for our existence. Without centripetal force we would be scattered all over the universe; without centrifugal force we would be pulled into the burning heat of the Sun. Only if we are well grounded in our everyday physical world, if we are able to experience ourselves as separate individuals, only then can we reach out to the universe without becoming uprooted. To remain ignorant of the mysteries of life may be to lose an opportunity to deepen our self-understanding and discover meaning in our existence.

The horoscope provides a clear structural framework within

which each group member can be given a unique and well-defined position. The psychotherapeutic work done in the group is being held by this structural frame and therefore can enter the psychic world reality in which there is only oneness and interconnectedness.

There are numerous ways of bringing synchronicity into the circles and using a horoscope to clarify and structure psychotherapeutic work. A variation on working with and around an individual horoscope is to draw a horoscope of the time when the workshop starts. This we call the 'group horoscope'. Each participant will represent one symbol during the whole workshop. We will explore how each astrological symbol coincides with the present life-story of its 'owner' and how the group horoscope actually describes the dynamics between the group members. Such a group, however, is not a closed system. It is a microcosm of society and therefore reveals something of the current problems of society. Similarly, a group horoscope can help to identify how a political event is reflected in the individual. We remember for instance workshops being held in Germany during the nuclear disaster in Chernobyl and during the time of the opening of the Berlin Wall. It was a remarkable experience, not to witness how these historic events affected the individual, but how they were symbolising, mirroring something happening within the individual on a psychological level.

The most adventurous work we have done so far is the family workshop. Again we draw a group horoscope and each group member takes on the role of one planet. We 'play' it only for a short while to get a feeling for the atmosphere of the horoscope. This we call the basic group structure. We then take each individual horoscope, one at a time, and treat it as if it were transiting the group horoscope. We want to see what happens when an individual enters the basic group structure. We trust that the way the individual enters the group and the way the group reacts to the individual will reflect his or her first experiences within a group: the family. In this work the focus is not on how a group/family is affecting the individual, but what an individual is doing to the group/family and what he or she is specifically needed for. We can see what impact one has had on the family, how the existing structure became transformed and how the family coped with the changes.

Working with Individuals

The idea of oneness and interconnectedness can be used without the help of a group and its dynamics, if two or more astrologers are interpreting a horoscope together on tape, without the presence of the horoscope owner. These interpretations then not only rely on the information provided directly by the horoscope and the intellectual understanding of it, but also on the information one receives by observing and interpreting the dynamics between the interpreters and whatever is happening during the interpretation.

We have analysed horoscopes together in this way, for individuals and for families, even over a span of several generations. Whatever is happening during the analysis, which can last between one and four hours, depending on whether it is an individual or a family, will be seen as a reflection of the horoscope and will be interpreted. Our personal feelings and life situation will then be observed and used as symbols resonating to the dynamics of the horoscope. In psychoanalytical terms we may call our responses 'counter-transferences'. However, this does not take away the mystery of the interconnectedness of our lives with that of the horoscope owner. To include the dynamics between the interpreters – if carefully and responsibly used – can open up a horoscope and its inner atmosphere considerably and can help the interpreters to *experience* and even live through difficult aspects, thus enabling them to comprehend and explain them much better. Often it is quite a remarkable experience to listen to a tape which not only describes but also, in part, re-enacts one's personal life-story (or that of a family).

5

CREATIVE ASTROLOGY, MYTH AND RITUAL

Helene Hess

Commentary

In the previous essay we read how it is possible to make use of synchronicity as a working tool of chart interpretation and of therapeutic intervention. People who for centuries, indeed for millennia, have been using what we now call synchronicity in a matter-of-fact way are ritualists; magicians, spiritual seekers and the priesthood, three categories which often overlap but are sometimes kept separate, as in our own day. Helene Hess here expands on the use of astrology as a framework for timing and interpreting ritual, which she describes as 'a ceremony with a spiritual significance'. Whether we take ritual simply as an operation for psychological rebalancing, as in the meditative exercises or indeed in the unconscious obsessive routines which people carry out in order to cope with the confusion of everyday life; whether we take it as the realignment of individuals or of a community with the Divine will, as in the rites of passage and the annual feast-days presided over by the major religions; or whether we take it more radically, as the invocation of a transpersonal force in order to affect earthly affairs more strongly than it or we could have done without the ritual; the ceremonies involved still form a bridge between the human world and the greater order which contains us. Helene's essay illustrates the use of the fixed stars, a framework little used in modern Western astrology, and their associated myths, for timing and interpreting just such a bridge-building ritual. This analysis repays detailed study, and may stimulate other people to use astrology once more as a means of ceremonial timing.

P. H. J.

In recent years astrology has made a big effort to find its way back to respectability. Efforts have been made to make its practitioners more professional in their counselling and there has been a lot of emphasis on the uses of astrology as a therapeutic tool. For some, to talk now of astrological interpretation in terms of ritual may appear to be a backward step. Astrology today may seem to have become somewhat divorced from these connections, but one cannot deny that throughout its long history astrology has had an association in one form or another with the religious or magical. One also cannot ignore the fact that there has recently been an increasing interest in the more mystical aspect of life. My own personal view is that astrology should not make the mistake of ignoring its own 'shadow', of becoming rigid in its outlook. Hopefully, as astrology itself has changed so much over thousands of years, it will be able to integrate and transform this area into something that is relevant to our own culture as attitudes and outlooks change.

According to the *Pocket Oxford Dictionary* definition, ritual is 'the prescribed order of performing a religious service'. This may conjure up the image of a traditional religious ceremony, but it can have a much wider meaning. I would say a fairer definition would be the prescribed order of performing a ceremony with a spiritual significance. Whether it be a pagan rite, a tribal ceremony, the service of an orthodox religion, or a ceremonial event at a 'New Age' gathering – the one common

86

denominator is that in one way or another there is a spiritual emphasis.

Having loosely defined the meaning of ritual, how can astrology be applied to it in a meaningful way? On a superficial level the religious and magical use of ritual could be looked upon as some form of group process and analysed as such. On both an individual and group level there are many areas which are relevant to the principles of psychotherapy – except that astrology goes one stage further and emphasises the importance of the spiritual in facilitating transformation, rather than relying solely on a counsellor or therapist. This is especially so in the area of the Western magical tradition.

Ritual can be performed for a number of reasons and on many different levels. It can be performed for oneself, usually with the intention of bringing about some form of inner or outer transformation. Rituals enacted for others are commonly used for healing or for initiation. Rituals can also be performed for the group itself, either as a festive celebration, or a re-minding or re-enactment of the archetypal teaching myths associated with a group of people's spiritual belief or deity. Finally there are rituals that are performed either by an individual or a group for the good of the collective.

It is extremely rare that a ritual intention is of a negative nature. Whatever the intention, the intended outcome is of a transformative nature. It is also generally believed by those involved that no matter what level the ritual is aimed at the outcome will, to a greater or lesser extent, affect all other levels. This may be based on the simple belief that awareness of those around us actually makes subtle changes to the greater whole through our own individual changes and actions, or, within a wider philosophical framework, the belief that by directing power from a higher source rituals have an effect on both the individual, humanity, and the Earth itself.

The Sun and the Moon are of particular interest as we already have a form of astrology still in existence as represented by the synodic year of orthodox religion and in the timing of many pagan festivals. Taking for instance Britain's traditional

87

pagan festivals which take place at the solstices, equinoxes and cross-quarter days, a lot of clues are given as to some of the deeper meanings behind the expression of solar energy within the zodiac.

With the Spring Equinox comes the first rising of the sap within the trees, at this time it is the celebration of the coming of spring, marking the change as the Sun enters Aries from Pisces. In May is the celebration of Beltain, the time of kindling the need-fire, when all fires were extinguished and a new one kindled. It is the time of the May Queen and the Maypole, symbolically representing the kindling of the seed in the womb of the virgin, or the fertilising of the Earth – all occurring within the sign of Taurus. At the Summer Solstice, the Sun enters Cancer from Gemini. It is the longest day, the Sun stands still awaiting its long return journey back into the Earth as it starts to move back towards the horizon in winter. All is at such a peak that the seeds of decline are present within the highest point of the light. Thoughts turn to the overthrow of perhaps an overestablished order within the knowledge that winter will surely come, a necessity if a new cycle of life in the next cycle of spring can be born in a future time.

Then comes Lammastide, traditionally associated with the ripening crops and things coming to their fruition when the Sun is in Leo. At the Autumnal Equinox the days are of equal length, when the Sun enters the sign of the scales, Libra, from Virgo. Things are held in the balance between the end of the summer and the first signs of winter. Quite a karmic symbol when the harvest taken in will measure the quality of survival through the long dark nights. The harmony between preservation and beauty and the beauty of the end of life as represented by the autumn, balanced against the destructive equinoctial winds of change. When the Sun is in Scorpio there is Samhain, or what is more commonly known as Hallowe'en. Traditionally the time when the ancestors are close to the veil between the worlds at the moment when the old Celtic year finishes and the new one begins. A period when amidst the decay of autumn there is hidden the hope of the sleeping seeds of another cycle.

In the midst of winter comes the festival of the Winter Solstice, and Christmas, the symbolic birth of the Child or the rebirth of the Sun as it reaches its lowest point in relation to the Earth, with the Sun entering Capricorn from Sagittarius. Finally this is followed by the cleansing tide of Imbolc, which represents the cleansing of the Mother after birth, returning her to her virgin state. The Earth in the northern hemisphere with the Sun in Aquarius is cleansed by winter's ice and weathering before the new growth cycle of spring.

Here we are talking of the cycles of growth. Similarly with the Moon. The new moon is the time for beginning things, the full for things that have come to their fruition and the dark of the moon a time for destruction and things of the dark. Again one can see the symbolic influence of the growth cycle. The new moon being in folklore a time of sowing, from New to Full is the time of growth of leaf and stem, and the Dark a period when roots grow, pushing their way into the soil.

Whilst the Sun speaks of things in the environment of larger inevitable cyclic changes that work from without to within, the Moon symbolises inner changes, or changes that come from within to without. Applied on an astrological level to a ritual enacted in the Western magical tradition, the Sun will indicate under what tide the ritual is being enacted, the type of power that is being generated in the environment and the point in the cycle of evolutionary growth. The Moon is the inner power that lies within the hidden levels of both ourselves and the otherworlds, symbolically represented by the menstrual cycle and conception. The interacting seasonal cycles of the Sun and the phases of the moon will indicate much about the energies that are channelled through the ritual and towards the intention of those taking part.

To illustrate this I have used the chart of The Four Blessings Ritual; a ritual that took place in Stroud as part of a weekend workshop called 'Magical Bridges' on 30 September 1989. I have chosen this one, as its framework is very typical. There is little room here to give the ritual's text but for those who are interested it can be found in Dolores Ashcroft-Nowicki's book, *First Steps in Ritual* (2nd ed), published by Aquarian Press. The intention of this ritual was to build a bridge between those present and the inner levels using the symbolic archetypes of the zodiac. In following this through, a circle of unity was formed with the light at the centre. As a symbol of higher unity this was enacted not only for the participants but also for the unity of humanity and the planet.

As can be seen from the chart in Figure 6, drawn up for the opening of the ritual, the Sun was in Libra in the 6th house. The Moon, also in the 6th house in Libra, was just past its fullness, but as it was over twelve hours past the exact solar opposition it could no longer be considered to be still in its full phase. In interpretation, the energies present coming from the inner realms represented the beginning of the dark destructive tide. The Sun in Libra also spoke of the energies of beauty and harmony at the end of a cycle and the preservation of balance for the changes to come. On a human level, in an air sign, it could be interpreted as the destroying of perceptual and notional barriers between people and the realisation that the seeds of harmony lie deep within all of us and are only awaiting the conditions for their growth. In the 6th house of service it is clear that this is a ritual of service to others, an astrological confirmation of the ceremony's intention.

Interestingly, the international situation between the Eastern and Western block, with the pulling down of the barriers by ordinary citizens within the Soviet Union, happened a few months later, surprising the world. This is not to say that this particular ritual had any direct bearing on events, but like the mysterious synchronicities that happen in astrology here was an outer event on a macrocosmic scale that reflected something in a concrete form of what was being sown at the time in the collective unconscious of humanity. This being reflected microcosmically within the ritual through the solar and lunar tides.

The framework of a chart in interpretation is also of importance (see Figure 7). The Ascendant as the rising

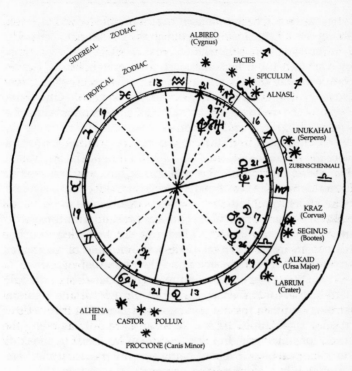

Fig. 6   'The Four Blessings Ritual'

point signifies the powers coming into the circle. It is the symbolic place of birth and the rising Sun. The MC, as the highest point, reflects the goals and aims behind the ritual and can be likened to the flowering of a plant that reaches towards the light of the Sun. Symbolising the downpouring of life-giving energies above and meeting with the upreaching growth below. The Descendant and any planet that is setting indicates what has been sown in the inner from the outer in order to bring about change. It is the place of the setting Sun and so too symbolises the point of death where the Otherworld meets this world. The IC, as the lowest point

91

beneath the Earth symbolises the roots and foundations of the ceremony, the material in which the seeds are to be sown.

Several years ago when I first looked at this form of astrology I was asked to interpret some charts for a series of rituals. It soon became apparent to me that the interpretive skills of ordinary astrology did not give a deep enough perspective. One could interpret the meanings of the planets within the signs and the tensions and flows indicated by their aspects. It was, however, clear that contemporary forms of astrological interpretation were geared more towards an individual personal analysis. I then realised with one foot in the astrologer's camp and another as a student of the Western Mysteries that a lot could be gained by looking further into the myths and symbols revealed by the planetary contacts in a chart of this nature. Certainly those who are trained in the Western Mysteries are well used to using symbolism and myth in meditation and ritual to gain a greater understanding of themselves and their spiritual legacy.

At the time I was also becoming interested in the use of fixed stars in chart interpretation. The tropical zodiac in Western astrology adjusts for the movement of the precession of the Equinoxes, shifting the zodiac from its stellar counterparts in the constellations. In my experience this tends to speak of the solar personal levels of being on this planet in the here and now. On the other hand planetary conjunctions with the fixed stars within the constellations of the sidereal zodiac give a picture of forces which colour the planetary energies affecting humanity as a whole and its connections with the planet and the cosmos.

In older forms of astrology the conjunctions of fixed stars to the angles and planets were often highly important to interpretation. The religious importance of the fixed stars is reinforced, not only by the deliberate use of myths of deities associated with the stars and constellations, but also by the fact that many temples of the Classical world were specifically aligned to the rising, culminating and setting of certain stars. Not to mention even earlier ancient megalithic sites in Europe and ancient Medicine Wheels of North America, many of

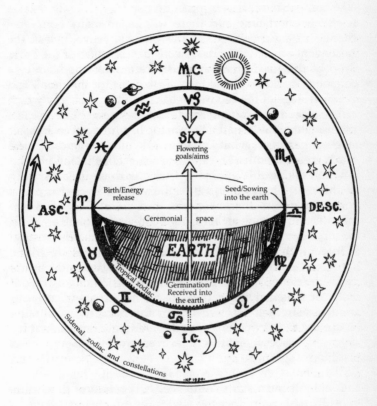

Fig. 7

93

which appear to be aligned to the heliacal rising of particular stars.

Using the fixed stars in interpreting a chart for a ritual or ceremony also has a very practical use. A ceremony takes a relatively short time and there will be no really noticeable change in the positions of the planets. Nevertheless the Ascendant and MC can move considerably against the back-drop of the fixed stars. A chart erected for the start of a ceremony could be likened to a birth chart for the ritual, and yet each stage of the ceremony has its influx of energy which can be picked up in an interpretation. If during the course of a ritual a note is taken of the time at the beginning of each major stage, a picture of what is rising and culminating can give a much greater depth of meaning to the actions taking place.

When taking this approach I usually draw up a list such as those in Figures 8 and 9 of the various stars that are in conjunction with the angles and the planets. Figure 8 lists in order the various stellar conjunctions to the angles in the example chart for each stage of the ritual. Each relevant star is listed with its constellation and magnitude, along with a short note on the figure or myth it is associated with. In this particular example I have used the myths and legendary figures from the Greek myths as they are the ones that are currently used in astronomy. However, for the purists it is possible to use the stellar myths from other cultures, especially if the myths are associated with a ritual event from the same cultural tradition.

There are a few points to take into account when assessing the strength of a star's influence. It is common practice to consider a star conjunct the angles, or a planetary body if it shares the same longitude as them. The longitude measures the longitude of the ecliptic, the imaginary path which the Sun and planets appear to follow in their movement across the sky, due to the effect of the planets moving in the same plane of orbit around the Sun. A star on the other hand can appear to the observer to be in a totally different part of the sky to a planet or the ecliptic and yet share the same longitude.

94

This is where one should take into account the magnitude and the latitude of a star. The higher the latitude of a star the further away it is from the ecliptic and therefore the further away a star is likely to appear from a planet. However, a star that has a strong magnitude and the same longitude as a planet, is still considered to be conjunct. The best rule of thumb is that a star has a strong influence if it has a high magnitude or if it is at a low latitude, especially if it is close to the latitude of the planet in question.[1]

Similarly a star sharing the same degree as the Ascendant or the MC may not necessarily appear to be rising above the horizon. As far as the Ascendant is concerned I will still interpret a planet as being conjunct if it is at the same degree of longitude, but also I take into account any stars that are at the mathematical point of rising. Vivian Robson's book *The Fixed Stars and Constellations in Astrology* gives a formula for this mathematical point which can be calculated quite quickly with the help of a good calculator. To evaluate when a star is conjunct the MC, rather than using the degree of longitude, it is best to use the Right Ascension of a star and divide it by 15 to find the sidereal time of its culmination, and then convert it into clock time.

In looking at the list of myths associated with each relevant star, one should begin to see a pattern of themes emerging. In the current example one of the most striking themes is that of healing, mortality and regeneration. There is a recurrent thread of associated myths running through the stellar contacts with the planets and angles (see Figures 8 and 9). The connecting factor is Apollo the solar Greek god of healing, prophecy and music. The rising of the Pleiades on the angles is associated with Artemis his sister and lunar counterpart, and so too is Ursa Major, a constellation that is connected with Mercury in the chart, Ursa Major as the Great Bear being one of her symbols. Mercury is also conjunct a star in the constellation of the Cup, Crater, which is also known as Apollo's Cup. The symbol of another cup is echoed through Altair, whose stars conjunct the MC at various points of the event. Altair's symbol

95

Fig. 8 STELLAR CONJUNCTIONS TO THE ANGLES

	Ascendant	MC
19.03/19.05 BST Opening and Cleansing of The Circle	Mathematical rising of *ALCYONE Mag. 3.3 and PLEIADES. Handmaidens of Artemis. Wives of 7 Rishis.	Conjunct *ALBIREO 3.2 Mag. in CYGNUS the Swan. Associated with Leda, mother of Castor and Pollux.
19.12 BST Calling in the light of the Zodiac	Conjunct *ZAURAK 3.2 in ERIDANUS. Meaning the Bright Star of the Boat Eridanus, the River.	*TARAZED 2.8 Mag. in Aquilla. Associated with Ganymede.
19.20 BST Circling of the Zodiac		*ALTAIR 0.9 Mag. chief star in Aquilla (see above).
19.25/28 BST Silent Meditation (focal point of the ceremony)	conjunct *ALCYONE and the Pleiades (see above).	*TEREBELLUM 4.8 Mag. in Sagittarius.
19.29 BST Giving of Symbolic Gifts	conjunct *ALCYONE and the Pleiades. (see above).	
19.46 BST Confirmation that the Work of the Ceremony was Completed		
19.47 BST Closing of The Circle		*PEACOCK 2.1 Mag. Associated with Argo the builder of the boat ARGOS
19.59 Finish	Conjunct *ALDEBARAN 1.1 Mag., the Eye of the Bull in TAURUS. One of the 4 heavenly guardians. The Watcher of the East.	

FOUR BLESSINGS RITUAL

Descendant
Conjunct
*ZUBENS-HEMALI 2.7 Mag.
and *ZUBEN HAKRABI 5.3
Mag. in LIBRA, both in the
Northern scale.

Conjunct *UNUKALHAI 2.8
Mag. in SERPENS. The
Serpent held by
Orphicus, the Serpent
bearer. Associated with
Asclepius. Conjunct Venus.

IC
Conjunct *PROCYONE 0.5
Mag. in CANIS MINOR.
Associated with Anubis.

Conjunct *CASTOR 1.6
Mag. and *POLLUX 1.2
Mag. in GEMINI.

Mathematical point of
setting *VINDEMATRIX 1.0
Mag. in VIRGO. A star
associated with the
harvesting of wine.
setting *ZUBENSHEMALI 2.7
Mag. in LIBRA (see above).

Mathematical setting
*ACRAB 2.9 Mag
the Crown of the
Scorpion in SCORPIO.

Conjunct *ANTARES 1.2
Mag., the Scorpions Heart,
in SCORPIO. one of the
four heavenly guardians.
The watcher of the West.

Conjunct *HAN 2.7 Mag. in
ORPHIUCUS (see above).

97

Fig. 9   STELLAR CONJUNCTIONS TO PLANETS IN
'THE FOUR BLESSINGS RITUAL'

Sun	No stellar conjunctions.
Moon	Conjunct *KRAZ 2.8 Mag. in CORVUS. CORVUS. The constellation of the Crow. Crow is the messenger to Apollo. See Aslcepius legend. Conjunct *SEGINUS 3.0 Mag. in BOOTES. Bootes the driver, hunter, or protector of Ursa Major, the Great Bear.
Mercury	Conjunct *ALKAID 1.9 mag. in URSA MAJOR URSA MAJOR. The Great Bear. Associated with Artemis and handmaiden Callisto. The Seven Rishis. King Arthur. Alkaid the home of Marichi, Queen of Heaven. Goddess of the Dawn in Tibetan Buddhism. Conjunct *LABRUM 3.8 Mag. in CRATER. Crater, the cup, associated with the Grail, the Goblet of Apollo.
Venus	Conjunct *UNUKALHAI 2.8 Mag. in SERPENS. Serpent held by Orphicus. Associated with serpent of Asclepius, god of healing.
Mars	No stellar conjunction
Jupiter	Conjunct *ALHENA 1.9 Mag. in GEMINI. Alhena placed in the foot of Castor, the mortal twin of Gemini.
Saturn	Conjunct *FACIES 5.9 Mag. in SAGITTARIUS. Nebula in face of Archer. Sagittarius associated with Chiron the Centaur, teacher to the gods and heroes, known for great wisdom, a healer and astronomer. Chiron/Prometheus myth.
Uranus	Conjunct *ALNASL 3.1 Mag. and *SPICULUM 6.0 Mag. in SAGITTARIUS. Alnasl marks the points of the Archer's arrow.
Neptune	No stellar conjunction.
Pluto	No stellar conjunction.

the Eagle is that of Ganymede, the human cup-bearer to the gods. Its conjunction with the MC speaks of the goals and aims of the group taking part, bearing for the gods the Ambrosia, of which only the gods can drink, the cup of immortality.

With the MC and Ascendant involved one is speaking here of the houses and angles. These define the ceremonial space

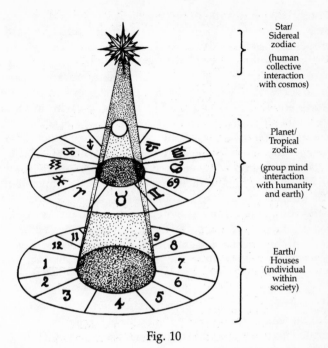

Star/
Sidereal
zodiac

(human
collective
interaction
with cosmos)

Planet/
Tropical
zodiac

(group mind
interaction
with humanity
and earth)

Earth/
Houses
(individual
within
society)

Fig. 10

and also symbolise the personal and individual interaction of those within the group taking part with society. This seems to be associated with the stages of the ritual involved with the light of the zodiac and perhaps indicates what sort of cup those in the group wish to bear for the gods, the cauldron and cup of the whirling zodiac.

With the entrance of an Artemisian force through the Pliades on the Ascendant, both at the beginning and at the peak of the ritual during the silent meditation, there is an indication of the type of forces being brought to birth. The Pleiades' symbol is that of doves, the symbol of peace. They were said to rise with the sun in the season when the seas became calm, here echoing the qualities of Libra, the sign on the Descendant and the sign that is reflected through the Sun and Moon via the tropical zodiac in this chart. The angles and houses represent the individual group interactional level of awareness, and the Sun and Moon as they have no stellar conjunctions, are reflecting the Libran energies of the tropical zodiac, and therefore are speaking less of a cosmic connection, than of an expression of energy associated with the group mind's interaction with humanity (see Figure 10).

Taking the most obvious points, Venus is conjunct a star in Serpens, the serpent held by Orphiucus, who is linked with Asclepius the god of healing and the son of Apollo. Saturn and Uranus are in conjunction with stars in the constellation of Sagittarius, which are said in myth to have been put there by the god Chiron, the renowned teacher and healer, and the teacher of Asclepius. Finally a star in the foot of Castor, one of the divine twins of Gemini, is conjunct Jupiter. Castor's story is that of his death through rivalry and duality. Apollo is implicated only in that Castor's killer took to wife a chosen love of Apollo's who jilted Apollo in the process. An event, though only part of a story, as in the Arthurian legends, is all part of the acts that lead to the death of the hero. Nevertheless Castor is reunited in the end and put amongst the stars through the love of his immortal brother Pollux. Both Asclepius and Chiron too had strange stories surrounding their deaths, even though they had the status of immortals. They too underwent death and yet eventually found their place in the stars.

Many of the stellar myths in Greek mythology relate to the granting of immortality through being given the honour of becoming a constellation. To be put amongst the stars symbolically seems to be speaking of the fact that those that are not of the gods are fated to be confined to the kingdom of Hades, the realms of Pluto. It is that which is beyond Hades planet, Pluto, which according to our known knowledge of the solar system is the region of the stars too. In other words, as a symbolic archetype, that which is confined within the solar system – that is, the Earth and the planets, etc – is mortal and subject to the laws of Pluto's transformations. Allegorically, that which is beyond this is the realm of the gods, which is enduring, the place of transformation of the spirit where different laws apply.

These tales are played out between the planets in the example chart. The most noticeable thing about the example chart is that all seems to be confined within a T-square between a Jupiter opposition to Neptune, Uranus and Saturn, and a square to the Sun in an exact conjunction with Mars and a very wide conjunction to the Moon. In terms of the stellar conjunctions the mythical Chiron is on one end of the opposition and Castor and Pollux on the other. These two myths hold opposite themes in their archetypal motifs. Castor and Pollux's very human story is that of duality in which a tale of rivalry and greed eventually results in Castor's death in a struggle with his enemy. Castor is the mortal twin having a mortal father and mother. However, Pollux cannot die as his father was the immortal Zeus. Pollux is so struck with the loss of his beloved brother that Zeus eventually breaks Pluto's claim to all mortals and recalls Castor from Hades, allowing the twins to be eternally united in the stars as the constellation of Gemini.

Saturn and Uranus, being conjunct a star in Sagittarius, represent the other end of the pole. Chiron, who is also immortal, is struck by one of Hercules' arrows. The pain is so great that Chiron begs Zeus to allow him to die. He offers to take the place of Prometheus, who, for stealing fire for humanity from the gods, has been condemned to a living death, chained to a rock, with his liver being pecked out daily by a vulture and dying at every sunset only to be reborn the next day. Chiron's is the ultimate sacrifice for humanity, for as Prometheus has suffered so has the human race, from the knowledge they have gained from Promethean fire. A clue to this legend is that Prometheus' name translated means forethought, the very ability that separates us from the animal kingdom, allowing us to invent – perhaps a mixed blessing, given those of our inventions that threaten the life of our planet. Hercules, too, is often seen as humanity itself. As he

101

too labours through the cycle of his twelve labours, so does humanity struggle to evolve.

Thus on one end of this opposition is the legend of how duality brings about death and an immortal reunion on a very human level, whilst on the other is the tale of the healer god who is wounded by humanity and is willing to die in order to free both himself and humanity of its pain. In this chart these are the backgound themes colouring the planetary energies, the motive forces that lie behind actions on the personal, material levels. Interpreting the sidereal zodiac is like looking at themes through a series of lenses. The constellations are always there, but their effects are focused by the stellar – planetary conjunctions which can be interpreted on a global level. As these are stellar conjunctions in the example chart, they reflect a universal condition of the very human Geminian dilemma of dualistic selfishness which is leading to the death of the lower self in opposition to a sacrifice of higher forces for humanity, all lying in the collective unconscious.

Taking this down to the level of the group taking part in the ritual of the current chart, we have the energy of the Geminian current from the star Alhena in conjunction with Jupiter. The Geminian quality will at the time be affecting the collective unconscious of humanity as a whole. Jupiter's archetypal energy represents our conventional social values, and the expansion of both the spiritual and the material through conventional means. It is the planet that represents where we have a propensity to expand, to develop the persona that is presented to society. The tropical zodiac sign Cancer is a protective sign, nurturing what it feels is its own and that which belongs to its ancestry, which will manifest itself in the group concerned at a group level. With all this occurring in the 3rd house, individuals within the group will be conscious of this energy expressing itself through ideas and communication. On a group level this suggests this is in the realm of ideas that are held onto and nurtured. With the influence of a Geminian star in the foot of mortal Castor this is the mortal part in the battle of duality.

102

Saturn sits on the other end of the opposition, in conjunction with Neptune and Uranus. The 'dweller on the threshold' of the boundaries between what we accept as ourselves and what we would prefer not to acknowledge as part of ourselves, confronting us with life's challenges in order to heal and teach. An appropriate position for the influx of Chiron energy, at this point in time when so much lies in the balance. Do we take responsibility for the Promethean fire? Our forethought has brought us to the very brink of realising that we are about to face a global crisis for what Promethean fire has brought us in our attempts to shape nature to our will. Saturn will not let us ignore the challenge, and yet within it is the very possibility of healing the rift between nations. If Prometheus is freed do we accept responsibility for the death throes and pain of a healer, teacher god whom we have accidentally wounded? For another aspect of the Centaur race is nature itself, in the beautiful bright face of Pan, whose name means All. Almost as a confirmation of this, his presence was felt by several members of the group within the ritual.

Saturn falls in the 9th house in conjunction with Neptune, and conjunct Uranus in the 8th, with all three planets in Capricorn within the tropical zodiac. The 9th house is the house of philosophy, religion and the law. Here we are speaking about the law and philosophy of Saturn as the 'Lord of Karma'. He teaches and heals us by confrontation with the pain of our past actions. Neptune's laws are somewhat different. These are the laws of dissolution. The dissolving of boundaries and the experiences of the mystic, who seeks union with the All and with God, and of sacrifice. In this chart Neptune is not conjunct any major star, and so reflects the energies of the tropical zodiac, Capricorn, which is at the group mind level. As such, Neptune's effect is nearer the level of the energies of the group taking part, and speaks of the breaking down of structures in a sign that tends to use structure as a means of reaching its goals. In fact the majority of those taking part were of a strong mystical leaning in the area of their philosophy and beliefs. With

103

the conjunction of Saturn we can see how the group energy within the ritual blends with the energies flowing through Saturn, with a concern for the state of the Earth being possibly a common meeting-point for those present. Added to this, with Uranus conjunct Alnasl and Spiculum, two more stars in the constellation of Sagittarius, another layer is added. Alnasl is actually placed at the tip of Sagittarius' arrow. Whether it is the arrow of the Centaur or that of Hercules, is another question, but Uranus' position in the 8th house of death leaves no doubt that its aim will be swift and sudden. On the level of the whole of humanity this was certainly the effect with the swift political events that took place between East and West. If this is happening on a planetary level, this is also happening within each one of us in one form or another on a microcosmic level. The weekend workshop where the event took place certainly used an alternation between right brain and left brain activity, with visual presentations of the material to be learned interspersed with a lot of information on the analytical level. Whether this brought inspiration or not to the majority of those present cannot be said, although there were a number of reports that this had been the effect.

At the apex of this opposition, is the square of Sun conjunct Mars in Libra in the 6th house which are not conjunct a star and so represent the personal levels. The harmonising and yet destructive side of the Libran solar tide has already been mentioned. This is further energised by the Mars conjunction, indicating the strong directiveness and single-mindedness of the group as a whole in the work that was being undertaken, directed on the personal levels in the 6th house towards the intention of service. As the fulcrum of the T-square and in the sign of the balance, it shows the tensions that were being generated between the stellar forces acting on the opposition. On a group level there were people present from many areas of belief and tradition, all were well aligned to the idea of service, but still there would be notional barriers as represented by Jupiter, in opposition to the urgency of the wider issues as reflected by Uranus, Saturn and Neptune.

The final point of focus of the T-square was the Moon, conjunct Seginus and Kraz. Seginus is part of Bootes, who drives, hunts, or guards Ursa Major, a constellation that has a lot of importance in stellar myths, one legend being that Ursa Major is the motive force that drives the universe around the Pole Star. This indicates the huge motive force that lies behind the lunar energy of Libra and the desire to serve in the 6th house. We also have another death regeneration theme in Kraz, part of the constellation of the Crow. It links with Asclepius, in that news of his mother's adultery was relayed to Apollo by the crow, which led not only to Asclepius' mother's death, but also to Asclepius' untimely birth. Here we again have the death of the old, this time in feminine form in order to bring about the new, a theme which is continuously repeated elsewhere in the chart, this time through the emotions and psyche, being the thankless task of the messenger.

How these manifest themselves within the stages of the ritual is interpreted in terms of the stellar conjunctions with the angles at each stage of the event. Castor and Pollux were actually conjunct the IC at the beginning of the ritual (see Figure 8). The IC in this type of chart represents what is beneath the Earth, and as the IC it is the material of the past, or in other words, the material in which the seeds shown by the ritual are to be received. Here it puts into perspective the more human problems of the battle between the earthly and heavenly Twins shown in Gemini. This battle is also reflected by Jupiter in the 3rd house of communication and ideas, which is conjunct Alhena in the constellation of Gemini. Here is where the group will, after the event, find the germinating seeds growing in their own development, and also will be a microcosmic reflection of what on another level is happening in the the whole of the macrocosm of humanity.

In looking at the movement of the angles there is no Sagittarian influence until the silent meditation at the peak of the ceremony. Thus the influx of Sagittarian energy is associated with the influx of power at the peak of the ritual where Terebellum, a star in Sagittarius, conjuncts the MC. In fact the MC, as can be seen in Figure 10, is important as a channel for the meeting of energy between the material level of the ritual enactment and the flow of energy coming from the hidden levels.

Another configuration belonging to this particular theme is Venus, conjunct Unkalhi, in the neck of Serpens, the serpent held by Orphiucus, the counterpart of Asclepius. In the 7th house this relates to relationships and partnerships with others. Venus, the planet of attraction and love, seen through the lens of the Asclepius theme, indicates the polarity between the healer and the healed. All the best healers seem to be able to use this polarising of energy in order to bring through the energy to heal. It also speaks of the higher love that urges the healer on to caring for and healing those that are sick. This has to be a love of a more universal kind to prevent too much identification with the patient.

Venus in the tropical zodiac is in Scorpio, a sign that Venus is not normally happy in, for it is the sign of deep aspects of sexuality, where the depths of love can turn to jealousy. However, it is also a sign associated with the Serpent. In Asclepius' case the Serpent is the Serpent of wisdom and healing. As such it may suggest that the depths have to be reached in order to bring about the wisdom to heal, as Asclepius was said to have done. When contemplating a serpent he had killed he learnt his healing art by watching the serpent's mate revive it with herbs brought in its mouth. This may suggest that the seed that was sown was the art of healing through the ray of love. But in learning that art, which can be healing on many different levels, an initiation must be undergone, in the form of a symbolic death. Although Asclepius was killed for his healing art, he was known as the twice born, for Zeus in his love for Asclepius, Apollo's son, raised him up again to be placed in the heavens in the constellation of Orphiucus. In relation to timing, it is interesting to see that Venus symbolically went beneath the Descendant when the circle was opened to the zodiac. Thus

106

this would seem to be the seed that was sown at the time in the material of duality as represented by the Geminian IC at the beginning of the ritual.

As demonstrated it can be seen how observation of the angles' stellar conjunctions is quite meaningful for an event like this. However, be wary of using the various interpretations of stellar conjunctions given for natal charts by figures such as Ptolemy which are usually of a very dire and exaggerated nature. They can be explored for their validity in an extremely watered down version for a personal chart interpretation, but in the case of ceremonial events of this nature it is more productive to look at the inner meanings of the myths associated with the stars and constellations concerned. Hopefully the Bibliography will help those interested in getting a head start. This area of astrology is very new to us and yet is also very old. There is great scope for creativity, and I have only revealed the tip of the iceberg here. For those who wish to research this further I strongly recommend learning about the fixed stars and their myths. There are many other forms of astrology, too, which may be very creatively explored here and perhaps once again it will be possible to bring back many areas of the ancient art that have been forgotten.

Note

1. Some astrologers also use parallels as well as conjunctions, but I have found the conjunctions alone are valid.

Bibliography

Ashcroft-Nowicki, D., *The Ritual Magic Workbook*, The Aquarian Press, Wellingborough, 1986

Bailey, A., *The Labours of Hercules, An Astrological Interpretation*, Lucis Press, 1982

Davidson, N., *Astronomy and the Imagination*, Routledge & Kegan Paul, London, 1986

Graves, R., *The Greek Myths*, Vols I and II, Penguin, Harmondsworth, 1975

Hinckley Allen, R., *Star Names, Their Lore and Meaning*, Dover Publications, N.Y., 1963

Lum, P., *The Stars in Our Heaven, Myths and Fables*, Thames & Hudson, London.

Robson, V. E., *Fixed Stars and Constellations in Astrology*, Aquarian Press, Wellingborough, 1979

=== 6 ===

UNLOCKING
THE HOROSCOPE

Prudence Jones

Commentary

Helene Hess has mentioned the role of the ceremonial space, the local sphere of the observer, in astrologically defining the roots and objectives of any given ceremony. My own essay in this collection discusses the use of creative methods and also of the 'creative space', whether ceremonial, artistic, therapeutic or other, as an intensifying, intermediate location between the vast and impersonal world of the macrocosm and the urgent, personal concerns of our own daily experience. It is rather like the solar station halfway between Saturn and the Moon in the traditional, Chaldean sequence of the planets. Here is where we are able to discover both ourselves and the universe through play, and here too is where we discover that we embody a greater order. The role of art as a mediator of the archetypes is often overlooked, and yet the artist, the visionary, and the contacted priestess or priest are not so far apart. To say this is not to build the ego of the artist, but rather to put his or her gifts in a greater perspective. It is a hint to those who are interested. The bulk of my essay is concerned with the way in which the absorbed concentration of the craft worker or artist has unlocked the mysteries of astrology and of personal psychology for people with whom I have worked.

P. H. J.

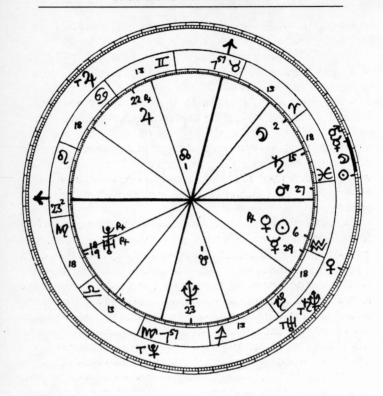

Fig. 11   A client's chart

'To work with the symbol, to observe it, contemplate it and use it, is to contact something of the nature of the planet itself. Without contacting that archetypal quality, new understanding of that planet is more or less impossible . . . To sense planetary energy is to touch the creative level.'

Cherry Gilchrist, *Planetary Symbolism in Astrology*

110

Every astrologer knows that moment when communication has somehow become inadequate and a bewildered client asks just what this or that feature of their natal chart means in practical terms, or just how some forthcoming transit is going to affect their day-to-day existence. It is the moment at which the concrete language of everyday life has shown its inadequacy for describing the trends and tendencies with which astrology deals. The keywords and rule-of-thumb generalisations have proved hollow, and we now have to find a new means of enabling our client to recognise the way in which their life is unfolding, to contact the essence of astrology in a form which makes sense in their own experience.

Figure 11 shows the horoscope of one such client. When she came to see me she was 23, an outward-going Aquarian, making headway in her job, though spending rather too much money on clothes, and more concerned with establishing herself in the career of her choice than with chasing any abstract ideal of personal wholeness. Specifically, she didn't want to 'get into her emotions', as the relative who had sent her to me had been happy to do in the sessions. However, when she came to see me, the Sun had progressed into Pisces a year before, and a progressed new moon was about to occur in that sign. Her teaching job had become less satisfying, and out of the blue she had fallen hard and heavily for a Cancerian man she had recently met when Jupiter transited into that sign. Integrating the emotions was precisely the challenge that was facing her then.

People with the Sun in Aquarius, in my experience, often find it difficult or inappropriate to express themselves emotionally. 'Not wanting to get into her emotions' here was a statement of character as well as the statement of resistance which a purely psychodynamic approach would take it to be. As astrologers, we can see that having only Saturn and Neptune in water signs, this woman might not find her emotions easily accessible, and they might very well seem strange and monstrous when she did contact them. However,

111

cool objective analysis would have distanced her from this newly awakened part of herself even more. What was the astrologer to do?

Perhaps imagery, the non-rational expression of the element of air, would help. I asked her how she felt in this situation. 'Like being tossed around in a stormy sea,' she said. Did she have an image of the sea? What colour was it? How high were the waves? and so on. The picture built up clearly. She was being tossed around by a powerful, raging flood, without tide or current, a force neither malevolent nor constructive, but completely indifferent to her well-being. I asked her in her imagination to switch to being the flood. Yes, the power felt comfortable, but there was no dialogue possible with the human being in the depths. Back as herself in the fantasy, my client decided it was better to drift and not let herself struggle. She found she was being dashed against something hard and crystalline. No pain or injury was involved; on the contrary it felt comforting. It was at least an anchor-point. Switching to imagining herself as the rock, she found she was very calm and stable. Her being reached down to the bottom of the sea, and she was quite unperturbed by the storm raging around her. Yes, of course the human being could shelter with her if she wanted to.

That felt like enough for one session. My client had discovered the stability of Saturn in Pisces, with its trine to Neptune in Scorpio at the depths of the IC. Furthermore, she had discovered it far more vividly and constructively than any way in which I could have described it to her. With that amount of emotional anchoring, she was able to spend the rest of the session discussing her newly awakened feelings without being terrified of them, and she began to gain some perspective on the man in her life, who until then had simply been an object of bewildered fascination.

She was also able to appreciate how her job, which had suited her airy temperament perfectly before the progressed sign change, now needed to involve more empathy, and she began to look for work which was a vocation rather than just a means of earning money. When I next spoke to her nine months later, she had long since dropped her obsession with the Cancerian man and had just finished an affair with a Sun in Leo man. He was married, and the affair had turned out to be going nowhere, but my client had been realistically enjoying the emotional experience for what it was, realising she would have to look elsewhere for a fuller partnership, without trying to turn this limited liaison into something it could never become. She was starting to make space for the emotions in her life.

The techniques of active imagination, role-playing, dance, painting and music-making, can help move us through the blocks we have which stop us from living out all that we could become. In sessions such as the one just described, creative techniques form a half-way house between the immutability of the planets in the sky, whose positioning can be interpreted but is far beyond our ability to influence, and the apparent freedom of choice that we have in our individual being. To be told fatalistically, that anyone with Saturn in Pisces in the 7th house can expect difficulty in achieving an emotionally fulfilling relationship, could easily have a devastating effect on a client, and no astrologer nowadays would do this. Alternative, though more optimistic, scenarios describing marriage to an older or more serious partner would, however, be equally partial, and therefore equally untrue. Astrology describes a more abstract reality than the particular objects and events of everyday life, and astrologers have the unenviable task of translating this abstract world into a language of particulars, the language which affirms our sense of free will or the ability to influence our world.

What actually was true for that client at that time was not only her objective situation of being overwhelmed by unfulfilled emotional longing, but also a symbolic reality, the image of the rock of stability, firmly anchored on the bed of the sea and so remaining steady despite the tempest raging around it. This might have been referred to her inaccessible, uninterested love-object, but in fact she interpreted the symbolism more constructively, as her own emotional stability, which of course it also was. Yet if the astrologer had initially interpreted the outer world situation in this way, describing the inaccessible love-object as a symbol of the client's own emotional steadiness and therefore as a helper in disguise, the reading would almost certainly have meant little and would perhaps have been downright insulting, appearing to 'blame the victim'. Most importantly, such an interpretation would not have helped the client deal with her situation. Her own creative interpretation, by contrast, did.

Why should this be? After some years of working with these techniques, I find it difficult not to conclude that our 'reaction' to planetary 'influences' (a turn of phrase which modern astrologers find quite unacceptable but have proved unable to replace) is always and necessarily creative. We are creatively interpreting our planetary blueprint at all times. We do not faithfully reproduce, automaton-like, the 'brute facts' laid down in the stars, because 'facts' on that level – the measurable astronomical data – are not of the same order as 'facts' on earth: the objects and events of daily life. Creativity is necessary in order for human beings to link the two. As we create our reality in the fantasies and role-plays of these sessions, so we see how we create, less obviously, less consciously, our reality in the outside world all the time. The creative embodiment of our natal charts goes on constantly, whether we are aware of this or not.

Every little detail in a session shows us expressing our planetary blueprint, and here the context of a group, rather than an individual session, allows these details to be picked up rapidly and interpreted effectively. For example, during a weekend workshop, a woman whom I will call Donna, wanted to explore her Saturn–Mercury contact. She sat and tried to express herself as Mercury, but to no avail. 'It's no good, I just can't do this; I just don't know what Saturn–Mercury means.' The whole group exploded in good-natured laughter, since Donna had demonstrated all too clearly precisely what Saturn–Mercury meant in that context. But the next step for her was to re-empower herself, to reclaim her Saturn and take responsibility for her silence. 'I won't just talk to any old person. I won't just babble on any old how like you people do. I'm not getting drawn. I'm here and I don't need you lot around me.' A powerful statement, and the group saw how her spine straightened and her feet rested more firmly on the floor as she took her stand. This role-play gave Donna the experience of how her private thoughts have always run along, unacknowledged, beneath the surface of outward sociability in which she had always forced herself to take part. She was vastly relieved by being able to share her underlying seriousness with others, to acknowledge it in public. Paradoxically this released her, for the duration of the group at least, to be more relaxed and chatty, knowing that now her inner seriousness had been acknowledged it was unlikely to disappear if she paid attention to the lighter areas of life for a while.

Creative Astrology sessions serve not only to show us how we are already living out the planetary archetypes, but also to give us the means of doing this consciously, to take responsibility for what we are already bringing forth, and thus to change it. An 'archetype', in esoteric jargon, is a pattern of reality which does not manifest directly here on earth, for it is not of the same order of being. It is always and necessarily translated into symbolic reality – and I understand symbolism (from the Greek *symbalein*, to throw together) as being the essential means of linking above and below, or as we may prefer to name them, abstract and concrete, general and particular. Astrological data give us an exact description of a general, abstract, archetypal reality which seems never to be reproduced literally in earthly affairs, but must be translated by means of symbolism into the particular, concrete, everyday reality of practical life.

Usually this richly creative process of symbolising is un-recognised by us, as in the case of Donna just described. Symbolism is seen as yet another description or observation from the outside, a static reality which merely confirms us in our stuckness, but in fact it is also a dynamic process in which we are totally engaged, it seems, at all times. To observe our symbolic reality from outside, as it were, to know as Donna did that Mercury–Saturn usually gives difficulties with communication, can be helpful, but, it seems, the observer mentality can easily induce paralysis. It is only by experiencing the creativity of our active interpretation of that symbolism at all times that we are released from the illusion of fate – determinism – which is engendered by all descriptive systems, from astrology through to neurophysiology. The free will that we then experience is of a different order from the absolute freedom of choice attributed to human beings by some opponents of astrology. It is the freedom to affirm what we are. To affirm what we are sometimes, paradoxically, liberates us from its confines.

One frequent pariah in astrological circles is the planet Pluto. Pluto's reputation for being heavy, controlling and withdrawn was modified somewhat when a workshop participant, whom I will call Brenda, chose to explore how trapped and inhibited she felt by the natal position of Pluto on her Ascendant. All her life she felt she had been a spectator, looking as if out of a dark cave at the colourful activity of other people's existence. The group arranged a makeshift barrier for her, a cave mouth of sorts, and Brenda began to explore her need to emerge. What did it feel like in there? Well at least it was safe, no one made any demands on her. However, life was cramped and unsatisfying in the cave, so Brenda started to make a move towards the outside world. But it was clear from her body movements that she was so used to making herself small and turning away from the world, that she had no idea how to go though the exit of her cave. There was an almost automatic revulsion from the freedom and expansiveness that would have been hers on the other side of the cave mouth. The whole group tensed up in sympathy. What was making Brenda so uncomfortable? Did she *have* to be uncomfortable? the facilitator asked. She was obviously used to living inside her cramped and sequestered

116

cave. Couldn't she let herself feel comfortable about doing so? Recognition dawned. All the muscles of Brenda's back and scalp relaxed and liveliness shone out of her eyes as she grinned at all of us, her Leo Ascendant visible at last. From there it was an easy matter to pick herself up and step forwards through the tiny cave entrance, stretching herself in the sunshine of the outside world in the confident knowledge that she could choose to step back inside her cave at any time she wanted.

In this case, Brenda's affirmation of what she was already doing, instead of making herself uncomfortable for doing it, released her ability to do it more consciously, and thus with greater control. As the Leo Ascendant showed, it was a case of becoming more wholehearted. At the same time, the quality of what she was doing changed. Heaviness, withdrawal and a feeling of being controlled turned into power and self-sufficiency, a quality of being which allowed her to revel in the sunniness and freedom of Leo, previously hidden by Pluto's darkness. Pluto tends to be cast as a 'bad guy', and so we often make him in our own unconscious interpretation of the archetype. We refuse to own and honour his potential, we refuse to clothe him in fitting symbolism. In the spacious world of the planetary archetypes, however, there are no 'bad' planets, there are no 'degenerate' aspects; there are just the abstract forces of the universe, which the ancients called gods and which we call archetypes, striving for manifestation in the life of each of us. We cannot manifest them constructively if we are afraid or ashamed of them, but by perceiving or experiencing them in their true undistorted form, we invoke a healing power. When such an outcast part of the psyche is at last recognised and granted its true place in its owner's life, it is finally able to 'play' freely and do its part in constructively creating the person's future.

The creative space of the workshop, consultation room or therapy group, a 'place set apart' which the Greeks called *temenos*, is a kind of half way house between the impersonal world of the planets – and indeed of other conceptual truths such as our knowledge of mortality – and the subjective sense of freshness and autonomy which we take with us into everyday life. In this intermediate world we can intensify our experience, shut out objective distractions and responsibilities, and also amplify our subjectivity by sharing it with others through drama, dance and discussion. Our modern *temenoi* are secular, places of psychological experimentation where miraculous happenings are called, non-commitally, 'synchronicities', but for the Greeks, the *temenos* was a sacred precinct, where the gods were invoked. In the modern context, by paying total attention to the creative process, we construct an environment where strange and transformative occurrences are likely to happen. The artist's studio too is a place set apart, and traditionally the process of artistic inspiration was attributed to a *daimon, genius* or Muse. All these beings were what modern transpersonal psychologists would call aspects of the higher (or deeper) Self of the artist, and indeed the true artist is the person whose higher (or deeper) Self speaks immediately to the instinctive awareness of a whole community. Religious rituals, carried on in a similar manner, recognised analogous but even more general beings, invited, invoked, but never controlled, as spirits or gods. By concentrating, within the sacred precinct or creative space, on our own process in accordance with a model of wholeness, such as the ancient pantheons or the modern pattern of the horoscope, at the very least we contact the part of ourselves that is at one with the archetypal formative process, and potentially we may invoke synchronicity, god/desses or miracles.

People often feel that their conscious will is pitted against the dictates of Fate. What we discover in the Creative Astrology session is that an unacknowledged part of us had been actively creating this apparent outside 'fate' all along, but without our conscious understanding. Strangely enough, by reclaiming responsibility for our creative part in this process, we are able to change its expression, consciously or else miraculously, and then by some mysterious means the planetary archetypes begin to manifest more constructively for us. In archaic terms, the gods need our conscious co-operation in order to show themselves to us in their benefi-cent guise.

My concern here, however, is neither with gods nor miracles, but with the more practical business of making the horoscope effective in personal reality. The unconscious creativity which seems to go on all the time beneath the surface of our awareness is especially apparent in our bodies. One exercise that was particularly effective when we tried it out in a workshop, and which I have found useful to practise at intervals since, is what Tina Whitehead, who originated it, called the Dance of the Elements. This is a circle dance in which a heavy, stamping step for the element of earth is followed by an energetic sequence ending in a leap up into the centre of the circle for the element of fire. Then an elegant, measured, serene section expresses the element of air, and finally a sinuous, rippling movement involving the whole length of the body from top to bottom represents the element of water. Everyone finds some elements much easier to dance than others. The exercise causes great hilarity and some serious resistance, but if people persist with it, they find that they become much more in tune with the qualities of all the elements in everyday life. The process of mastering each step in a single workshop eventually releases the element(s) which are most strongly emphasised in a person's natal chart, and this can be a shocking experience for people who have forced themselves to live in a situation which is alien to them: 'out of their element' quite literally. To learn the dance and do it at regular intervals is a profoundly healing exercise, which rebalances us naturally and can draw us into a more appropriate way of life without undue trauma. Be warned that this exercise seems to arouse a strong resistance in the form of 'forgetting' or becoming unaccountably reluctant to do it. People seem to be strongly attached to their specialised routines of movement.

It is also interesting to combine the dance movements

with sound: a *basso profundo* growl for Earth, a war-whoop or a shout for Fire, the clear, mellifluous spoken diction or recitative of Air, and the lyrical head tones of Water. Again, we find that we can use our voice in certain ways far more easily than in others, and that attempting to release the missing tones can bring up a strong emotional reaction and memory of how the missing function was lost. Curiously enough, these sounds fall physiologically into two groups, one linking the complementary opposites Earth and Fire, which both emphasise the use of the so-called 'chest' voice, and the other linking Air and Water, traditional opposites whose sounds specialise in using the so-called 'head' voice. Traditionally, Earth and Fire are different ways of *being*; Air and Water different ways of *relating*. Physiologically, the chest voice is produced by laryngeal muscles which tense and relax by themselves; the head voice on the other hand by a membrane which comes into operation only when stretched by other, supporting muscles. The muscles of the chest voice are self-sufficient; those of the head voice function only in relationship. However, this whole area of the use of the voice in astrological symbolism needs further exploration, and it might yet be found that these sets of sounds do not spontaneously express the elements for a majority of people.

'Dancing the horoscope' is another revealing exercise, which relies on the symbolism of the four cardinal points. We can interpret the horoscope's Midheaven as corresponding to the head on the physical body, the IC as referring to the feet, and the Ascendant and Descendant as symbolising the two hands (see Figure 12). The distribution of planets around the four quarters of the horoscope can then be expected to delineate different centres of energy in the body, and the dance makes these centres dynamic, so that they can express themselves more effectively. Just as airy people find creative techniques of imagination easy to use, so fiery people tend to go for the movement exercises.

Unfortunately this exercise had not been developed at the time I worked with a dynamic Leo individual whose

120

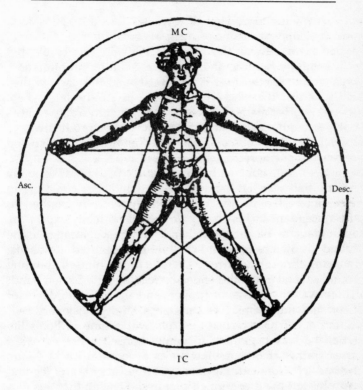

Fig. 12   Correspondence of the chart to the physical body

horoscope fitted the physical model in a striking way. All his
planets except one were above the horizon with the Sun at the
Midheaven, and he had made good use of this pattern, having
a successful and prestigious job. His Sun in Leo and Moon in
Cancer corresponded well to his feeling – and appearance –
of 'having two different eyes, a hard one and a soft one';
but the important and unresolved feature of the horoscope
was the single planet in the northern hemisphere: Saturn
retrograde in Aquarius at the IC. This person had been born
with crippled feet – unconscious, that is, prenatal, 'creativity'

121

in a harrowing form. He had worn leg irons until he was 10, and had only the faintest memory of life before that age. When I worked with this man, his feet were serviceable, but still painfully twisted, and highly resistant to interpretation, creative or otherwise. It is in precisely such a case as this, with Saturn, the blocker, retrograde in an air sign, where the non-verbal method of letting the body physically express itself through movement and dance might be productive.

'Dancing the horoscope' confirmed an intuitive hunch and released a memory for another fiery type, a Piscean artist, whom I'll call Bob, with Jupiter in Leo rising. Like many artists, Bob was left-handed, and he and the whole group were interested to find out which hand corresponded to the Ascendant in his chart. We would normally expect the Ascendant to be the right hand. At the beginning, as he found his own balance and rhythm, Bob reported, it was like 'dancing through a mirror'. Then he found himself spinning round several times and ended by leading with his left hand. There was the power of Jupiter, and the self-confidence of Leo, showing themselves through a kind of visionary self-sufficiency. This exercise took place at a time in Bob's life when he was beginning to define himself seriously as an artist, rather than pursuing art as a vocation in the hours he had left from earning money. The experience of leading with his left hand confirmed him in the feeling that this was the correct decision to take, and he remembered a time years before when he had been working as a salesman, once more to earn money to keep his family. His boss had taken him aside one day, and asked if he really enjoyed selling. 'Oh yes, of course, I'm very keen on the job.' 'Now come off it, you're not really. What really makes you enthusiastic?' Eventually the boss persuaded Bob to admit that his true love was painting, and like the intuitive that he too presumably was, said, 'Well, you should do what you're enthusiastic about. You'll never make a good salesman if your heart's not in it. Now go and make a go of being an artist.' Although Bob hadn't actually done that at the time, these words flashed into his memory when he was dancing. The experience felt like a very deep confirmation of who he was.

Bob's experience of dancing his Ascendant through his left hand rather than his right illustrates what is in a sense the research application of creative techniques. Astrologers usually verify their astrology by observation of what clients do and what they experience in the normal business of everyday life. Every working astrologer builds up a stock of informal observations, as does every GP and every counsellor. Organised statistical research too, of which counsellors and GPs have plenty to draw on, but astrologers considerably less, simply describes more rigorously what it is that people happen to do in everyday life. However, astrology is not simply an applied science; it is an interpretation of the world, as for example are religion and art, and it has also had a significant input from trance mediums and intuitives, who are 'given' their data while in an altered state, directly from the visionary mind and not from observation of the outer world. Creative astrology now extends such faculties to all. This does not mean that every student in a workshop will turn out to be a gifted visionary, far from it. It does, however, mean that working astrologers, and organised psychological researchers if they wish, now have the tools for awakening the visionary or intuitive faculty – the 9th house area of the mind – which exists, to however limited an extent, in all people.

This gives us access back to what I have called the arche-types. From our half way station, our creative space between the worlds, we cannot only intervene in the way in which we spontaneously act out the archetypes in practical life, by altering the symbols in which we clothe them. We can also contemplate the symbols themselves, not in order to improve our personal situation in the outside world, but in order to allow the inner archetypes to clothe themselves in different symbols, to adapt themselves to our time. This is what visionaries have always done: they have reinterpreted the eternal patterns of the gods in a form intelligible to human beings at a particular stage in history. Thus in Bob's case, the overall intention was to free workshop participants' physical expression of their planetary pattern, an individual and practical task. But the spin off was an observation about how the horoscope was embodied unexpectedly in one particular left-hander, how the archetypes which the planets represent were symbolised spontaneously by his physical being. This was a general and theoretical observation, which invites further investigation by other left-handed people to determine whether they generally express their Ascendant through their left hand, or whether Bob's reaction was simply his individual creative response to the task of embodying the horoscope. Doing this sort of research, we are able to update and rewrite astrological theory.

For instance, the problem of house systems is a knotty one which astrologers this century have tended to avoid. I have written elsewhere about the theoretical basis of house systems (see Bibliography) – a rational 9th house activity – but most other research has been based on the 3rd house method of observing what people experience when planets happen to transit or progress across the variously calculated house cusps. Now, however, it seems we have the tools to supplement these approaches by the non-rational 9th house method of creative exploration. Here is an example.

During a workshop on the houses, participants were guided through the visualisation of a round table, the circle of the zodiac, at which a representative of each planet was present. The planets were seated according to their house placement in the person's horoscope, and the aim of the visualisation was for each person to discover which planets they got on with easily and which not, observing the quality of the interaction in each case. The usual question of which house system to use came up, and participants were told to adopt whichever system they usually used, to see how the different methods compared.

The contrast in the Equal House system between the Midheaven and the 10th house cusp came out clearly in the experiences of one astrologer, a Taurean with the Sun,

124

Mars and Mercury in the 10th house, but Jupiter and the Midheaven in Pisces in the 9th. Which was his true career significator? The Sun and Mars looked 'a bit awesome, a long way over there', he reported. He didn't feel much in common with them, but Jupiter, sitting over on his left in Pisces, radiated benevolence and even offered to act as a mediator between him and his Sun. The Piscean Midheaven for this person signified his aspirations. 'If I had the time I'd just lock myself up in the attic with my books and my crystals', he said fervently, but as it was, like many of his Taurean tribe he earned his living as a telephone engineer, exercising his undoubted skills and gaining self-esteem, but not fulfilling his need for a vocation.

Notice that despite the Sun's being in the 10th house, this person did not identify with the affairs of this house. On the contrary, the Sun seemed distant from him. This is not unusual; people often report that they are cut off from the Sun, the basic drive for significance in life, but here the experience was complicated by the competing claims of the Sun's stellium and Jupiter to determine the horoscope owner's public persona. In fact, Jupiter and the Midheaven clearly took over the role of parent figure, as is often shown by the Midheaven; but the 10th house solar stellium in fact described this individual's choice of career, the public face he showed to the world. His emotional energy was in Jupiter, but he was not himself Jupiter. His career energy was in the Sun, but he did not identify with the Sun either. Notice that his dilemma carried the seed of its own solution; the kindly offer by Jupiter to act as a mediator. This was to be taken up in future sessions, with an aim to easing the dichotomy.

Such techniques, meditative and role-playing, are quite fascinating as a means of research, of contacting the principles behind the various astrological features such as planets and angles. For example, there is a long-established Neoplatonic tradition of the 'harmony of the spheres'; the perfect sound which the planets are said to make while moving in their orbits. As modern biophysics is now corroborating ancient traditions about the influence of sound, both creative and destructive, on the material environment, the imagined sound of each planet, subjectively experienced, is an interesting field to explore. In many groups now people have contacted the vibration of their ruling planet within them and have hummed or otherwise resonated its tone, allowing it to express itself spontaneously through them. Curiously enough, a group humming the note of their ruling planet, the ruler of the Ascendant, always sounds far less harmonious than a group humming the note of their Sun-sign ruler, and most individuals feel more at home 'tuning in' to their Sun-sign ruler than they do to their Ascendant ruler.

Once more, we can follow up this finding in two ways. The first is the more urgent business of exploring how each individual voices or expresses these two planets in their life, so that they can learn to do so more effectively if they wish. The second, however, is the long-term theoretical enquiry as to whether people are generally more naturally in tune with their Sun-sign than their Ascendant, whether this finding holds true in groups which are not steeped in popular Sun-sign astrology, and so on. Creative Astrology is extremely exciting as a means of tackling both these questions.

By applying the techniques of humanistic psychology to astrological interpretation, then, people are able to unlock many of the blockages that we all encounter in expressing our planetary potential easily and effectively. In this process we seem to encounter a persistent stream of creativity, often unacknowledged by the individual, which appears to function constantly beneath the surface of our everyday awareness. Bringing this creativity into consciousness is a key to energising the abstract information of the horoscope so that it can be useful in a person's life, a process traditionally known as invoking the archetypes. In addition, by paying attention to the form of the symbols that we spontaneously produce in these exercises, we can expand or modify our comprehension of the archetypes that we understand as lying behind them, we can all, whether natural trance mediums

126

or not, gain a deeper understanding of the concepts which motivate astrology.

By making this creativity playful, open-ended, rather than goal-directed, within the safe confines of the 'creative space', we seem in some way to invoke a spontaneous, unexpected power of resolution from outside, a healing synchronicity which is not under our conscious control, cannot be aimed at, analysed or bidden at will but merely trusted to appear through our utter absorption in the details of creative expression. This seems to be an informal, non-specialist version of the creative process gone through by talented artists, whose creations speak to all of humanity. It is also a modern, humanistic form of the ancient sacred process by which the gods, which we nowadays call archetypes, were invoked within the temple precinct, the 'place set apart', in order to realign and inspire human actions in accordance with the objective will of the heavens.

Bibliography

Gilchrist, Cherry, *Planetary Symbolism in Astrology*, London, Astrological Association/Saros Foundation, London, 1980

Jones, Prudence, 'Celestial and Terrestrial Orientation' in Annabella Kitson, *History and Astrology: Clio and Urania Confer*, Unwin Hyman, London, 1989

RUNNING LARGER CREATIVE ASTROLOGICAL EVENTS

Palden Jenkins

Commentary

Hans Planje and Jochen and Ulrike Encke have already shown us how current astrological themes can be embodied within a group of people. Palden Jenkins goes a step further, into the public realm of the community or small village. He works deliberately with large groups, setting up a context in which whatever happens can be seen to embody the interrelationships of the planets. His Living Astrology camps are not primarily therapeutic, but are educational events for the participants, and experiments in astrological discovery for the organisers. When 60–120 people, astrologically classified, interact in an outdoor gathering, interesting generalities emerge and interesting synchronicities occur, which can be placed in the context of the astrological cycles which are visible among the stars at night and can be sensed by mood swings and energy fluctuations throughout the camp. Here the astrological context extends beyond the purely human realm of psychology and social structures, to the natural world of weather, health and the fertility cycles of animals and plants. Participants find that they are knowingly living out the objective cycles of time, an experience which is less accessible in fragmented city life or even in the intensely personal context of a therapy group. Palden's essay sets out the guidelines for organising a Living Astrology event, and describes the results of some previous ones.

P. H. J.

The wonderful thing about bringing larger numbers of astrologically interested people together – and here I am talking about sixty-plus people – is that they have wonderful ways of dividing into subgroups, and interacting with one another in all sorts of permutations, working with specific, identifiable energies. I have run educational events for people in several different subjects (prehistory, music and dance, crafts, healing, magical–spiritual work), and in terms of group process, astrologers have been the most exciting participants of all.

An additional advantage with astrologers is our work with an interesting mix of the theoretical and the experiential, allowing dimensions and techniques of group process not easily available to other interest groups. In other words, it is possible simply to call out, 'Everybody in their Mercury groups!', and within a few minutes you have twelve groups of people, who can discuss an astrological or life issue together, go into personal sharings or work through experiential processes.

One can subdivide the whole group into two (gender), three (mode), four (element), six (polarity) or twelve (zodiacal sign or house) subgroups with very little difficulty – and, what's more, all of the members of those subgroups will have a real affinity and energy relationship with each other. Permutations vary from gathering to gathering, with certain signs or patterns predominating at one time, and changing at another. This can have its disadvantages, for you can land up with fifteen Leos and one Piscean (or vice versa!): since these gatherings involve growth and initiation, all people who are there have come (by magnetic attraction) because they are somehow *meant* to be there. So, in this matter, we take the rough with the smooth!

Teaching, public speaking and running group events have come naturally to me since I was 13. When transiting Uranus and Chiron squared my natal Virgo/9th Sun, at the age of 34, I found myself suddenly running weekend gatherings, at Glastonbury, in South-West England, where I lived. It all just *happened*, unexpectedly successfully. As time went by, this led to more gatherings, and then to longer-lasting outdoor camps, and I found myself, with the many other fine souls who joined in, growing in experience and understanding of larger-group process. Eventually, in 1986 (on my third Pisces/3rd Jupiter return, and with Uranus and Chiron now squaring my Virgo/9th Saturn) I realised I needed to found a proper organisation to work with this educational evolution, and thus the Oak Dragon Camps and family came into being, now continuing (mostly without me) to run camps around England and Wales, covering a range of subjects and slants, and making gradual moves towards charitable and transnational status.

Gathering Together

From the beginning we were seeking to call together a wide spectrum of astrologically interested people, from 'cottage astrologers' to urban association members, and to give them an opportunity to interact with each other in an 'unstructured-structured' way. The principle of this format is that we invite experienced teacher-facilitators to share their favourite material, and to act as 'resource-people', responding flexibly to expressed needs and requests from the assembled people. We also give space for any participants to suggest specific things openly, or to take initiatives. If these are not forthcoming, we operate a fallback programme devised by the organisers and teachers' team. But this has rarely been necessary!

Each day is divided into periods – morning, afternoon, evening, with provided meals and free time in between.

Different periods are given to different kinds of activities – lectures, discussions, sharings, experiential sessions, or small groups – or to spontaneous arisings. Then, with attention more on influencing *method* than to steering *content*, we let people ferment together in study, fun, experience and discussion. This is done with a degree of control, and a large degree of freedom-giving. The subtle balance between these poles is found through experience and skill-development – and I've found that a facilitator needs to be ready to lay himself or herself on the line and work publicly with power issues with the best motivation and receptivity possible. Everyone is a part of everyone else's personal process. 'It's not what you get for it, it's what you become by doing it' (John Ruskin).

What often happens is a series of group 'miracles' – something infinitely more potent than first expected. Everybody seems to find what they need, plus more, and is empowered and enthused to make great further progress at home, not only in astrology but also in the resolution of crucial life issues. It's a high-risk game for the organiser and facilitators, but deeply rewarding. The main pay-off is the joy of playing an active part in synergistic breakthroughs, personal and group empowerment, and being part of an immense collective spiritual lift. It also transports astrology out of the head and off the bookshelf, into people's own hands.

Being fired by larger numbers than in an ordinary-sized astrological or therapy group, the experience becomes exponentially stronger and deeper. The optimum number for such events seems to be 60–100 people: the issue is to enable everyone to be able to look into each other's eyes and say 'I recognise you'. Collective alienation patterns emerge, however, if the group numbers more than 120 people, and individuality and intimacy can be lost: large numbers might be commercially more attractive, but qualitatively, they detract from collective growth.

In my experience, the optimum duration of a gathering is a minimum of three days and a maximum of ten. This gives enough opportunity for everyone to settle in, for the Timeless to creep in, and for people to get lost in the subject and situation for a while. I find the optimum space to be one where there is little outside distraction, where self-consciousness melts forgetfully, and where there are enough flexible larger and smaller space-opportunities for whole-group and small-group needs. It helps to be in a greenish or rural location, or at least in one where there are opportunities for quietly escaping from others or having tête-à-tête meetings in corners.

However and wherever I have run an event, I've paid careful attention to both environmental and facilitation factors – and to allow for unpredictable 'Factor X', outer planet influences too!

Silence and Pow-Wow

Two keys to a successful gathering are good facilitation and inspired application of conscious group dynamics. The facilitator needs to be someone with a loud voice, aptitude, clear motivation and some experience. Two tools I have found crucial to positive group dynamics are: (1) Silent Circle, and (2) what we have come to call 'Pow-Wow' (although in the USA, out of respect to native Americans, I call it 'All-Thing', a Scandinavian term for a moot).

Silent Circle is important at the beginning, at critical punctuation points throughout the gathering, and at endings. Method: everyone gathers in a circle, comfortably, holding hands (optional), and remains silent for a period of minutes. Silence is something everybody everywhere does in the same language. It allows the group to pause from its chatter and doings, to meld and to receive. Silence offends no one, and unites everyone in their basic humanness.

In Pow-Wow, everyone present sits in a circle, and is given the opportunity to speak and be heard. The Pow-Wow can either be chaired (best for efficiency, decisions or information-sharing) or a talking-stick can be used (best for personal sharing, creativity and spontaneity). It can also be conducted by 'freeflow' (no rules), but this requires a mature, experienced group who have generated the strength and solidarity to allow pauses between contributions. If the talking-stick is employed, the instigator needs to outline clearly the few 'rules' of Pow-Wow first, then to place the talking-stick in the centre. The first person who is moved to contribute takes the stick, and when finished, passes it left or right, so that it gradually moves around the whole circle.

The talking-stick enables everyone to give complete and utter attention, while the holder contributes in words, song, silence or action, until they feel they have finished. As the stick moves round the circle, remarkable things can arise. The main outcomes can be feedback, creative suggestions or commentary, group bonding, profound sharings and breakthroughs, and spiritual uplift, generated by everybody, together. People start contributing on each other's behalf. We begin understanding that all our problems are one at root, and that we can help each other use our fears and doubts to help us move forward.

This gathering format is obviously very different from a standard conference, where rows of chairs face the stage, programmes are adhered to tightly, and interactive processes are restricted to breaks, meals, corridors and question times. The genius of speakers is witnessed, but participants are cast in the role of learner, while teachers get stuck in the role of expert! Conferences and gatherings each have their pros and cons, yet the availability of both would benefit everybody in the astrological community (except perhaps recluses!).

'Processes'

During a Pow-Wow at a Glastonbury Living Astrology Gathering at Easter 1985, a remarkable thing happened. It arose through the mouth of one individual (perhaps the group's Chiron manifestation![1]), but in a sense it was a message from the whole assembled eighty-strong group – and perhaps a cry from the collective unconscious of all astrologers! The person who proposed it was a punkish, early-twenties non-astrologer, who was innocently making what he expected to be an inconsequential suggestion. In such ways new waves are born!

He had understood our recommendation to learn astrology in direct conjunction with living life. He felt a need to meet with other people of his own Sun sign, to find out how they experienced their own lives. So he suggested that we all subdivided into Sun sign groups, to compare notes on the issue – which we duly did. This turned out to be so successful, so simple and obvious, that it became a core practice of the gatherings and camps, generally known as 'Processes'.

For processes we have arranged the floor or ground as a zodiacal circle (using flags, floor-marking or simply chairs with paper zodiac signs on) amongst or around which people sit: this gives a clear frame of reference for everyone. If a large proportion of beginners are present, everything needs to be well explained and kept simple – for it is surprisingly easy to create confusion in a large group! A facilitator (plus an assistant) starts the process by outlining a few ideas and images to help people get going – without defining things too closely. Everyone gathers together, then subdivides into their planet groups, and these groups are given a period of time in which to share experiences (10–40 minutes, depending on numbers and timings). The facilitator then wanders around the groups, helping them make progress (without teaching or giving answers) and calls 'time!' when appropriate.

Afterwards, several things can happen: (1) a spokesperson from each group can share a verbal review of what the sign-group uncovered, before the whole circle; (2) each group can devise and act out a cameo or situation which to them creatively exemplifies their sign and its patterns, for the rest of the circle; (3) each group can paint a group painting (requiring materials) or write a record of their discoveries together. Another variant is to present problems to the groups, to

134

find out how they would deal with them. For example, in Moon groups, 'How would you react if you went home to find your house had been accidentally demolished?'; with Saturn groups, 'How would you feel if you were arrested without apparent reason, and had to answer to the kind of heinous accusations you most fear?'; or with Jupiter groups, 'What would you do if you found that you had unexpectedly inherited a million?'

In all cases, feedback to the whole group at the end of subgroup sessions is important, in that it allows everyone to learn from everyone else. The facilitator needs to keep this moving (with time in mind), and perhaps point out similarities between groups of the same element or polarity, or themes which are emerging, which deserve to be under-lined or interrelated.

The wonderful thing is that these interactive processes are valuable for everyone at all stages of learning astrology – from beginner to expert. It reaches beyond mere reiteration of established astrological concepts. As in Gestalt groups, everything which happens in such groups is relevant – including the way people sit, the ease or lack of communi-cation, the hidden agendas, or even 'offstage' noises, for we are not dealing with theoretical situations here: such groups represent a living massing of particular astrological energies. A magic starts moving.

It takes between one and two hours to run a process. In a consecutive series of such sessions it is possible to move through interactive processes for each of the planets. At the camps, we spent an afternoon each day with each of the personal planets, Moon to Saturn, over a period of a week. It could be done with a dedicated large group meeting once weekly however. Outer planet groups usually become too large, concentrated in but a few signs, and hazy in their focus, but it is conceivable to run such groups fruitfully in the right circumstances – perhaps more experientially than verbally. It is also possible to work through planets in natal houses, in a separate set of processes.

135

Each planet-process naturally evokes a different atmosphere: exploring lunar energies creates a contrasting ambience to Mars energies – and we have found that Mars and Saturn groups in particular need running competently, positively and at the 'right' time.

It's also possible to run 'Transit' or 'Aspect' processes. In Transit processes (involving transits by Saturn, Chiron, Uranus, Neptune or Pluto to chosen natal planets) groups can be formed to investigate either transiting or transited planets. With Aspect processes, a similar group-arranging procedure can be used to create groups which investigate either natal planetary pairs (for example, Moon–Jupiter, Venus–Saturn or Sun–Pluto) or certain types of aspects (say, hard or soft aspects to Jupiter, Saturn or Pluto). I have found that the best way to do this is to ask everyone to select a major outer planet transit which is current for them (within a year of the present), with encouragement to choose intuitively if they have a choice to make. When this is done, certain transits will become clearly apparent as common to many (Saturn returns, Pluto–Sun transits and others), and with deft arrangement, other groups can be formed to cover, say, Neptune transits to Moon or Venus, any outer planet hard transits to Saturn, or Chiron transits to any natal planet. When everyone is catered for, the process proceeds.

Note that if each subgroup, in its sharings, notes its findings, or runs a (preferably small and inconspicuous) tape recorder during the feedback sessions, it is possible for someone with editorial skills to compile a book of observations which is drawn from a wide consensus of sources. It is surprising how many new perspectives arise through these interactive processes, and how many old astrological concepts are invalidated or modified in this empirical 'opinion poll' method.

What has surprised me most in the results arising from astrological group process, is the extent to which our knowledge is book-based, rather than experience-based. The planet-in-sign groups reveal anomalies such as weak and self-doubting Leos, chaotic, incompetent Virgos, shy Sagittarians and Aquarians who hate groups. I have sat in horrific silence with twelve Gemini–Moon individuals, have noted the weak positioning of Uranus in the charts of many astrologers, and have heard some people reporting the hardness of Neptune transits, while others describe the softness of Pluto ones! Although these are minority observations, they have been, for me significant ones, underlining the fact that a sign, house, planet or aspect refers to a field of distinguishable possibilities, and standard images such as the nit-picking Virgo or the woolly Pisces represent but one expression of each of these features.

More orthodox situations can be interesting as well. I have sat in a Venus–Leo group where nobody could get off their pedestal to allow a fruitful interaction to occur – no one would lead, no one would follow, no one would get together as equals. Paradoxical was an experience in a Gemini–Moon group, where we couldn't strike up a meaningful conversation on anything at all – yet we changed our strategy and landed up having tea and cakes at the café! It can be interesting when such groups are set to work. At one of the camps we asked Ascendant groups to participate in turn in helping out in the kitchens and site work: the kitchen staff fed back that the Virgos were really difficult and disorganised, and the Aries people scrubbed the place clean! Draw your own conclusions! Often such interactive processes throw new light on astrological assumptions, expectations and fixed ideas. They can also throw light on the nature of the time: one sign might be thrumming well, while another might be stumped, silenced or troubled.

Horoscope Weaving

A briefer version of the processes is 'Horoscope Weaving'. For this we have used a largish zodiacal circle on a floor or ground surface – at camps we had a big circle of flags,

137

coloured by element, with Aries east, Cancer north, Libra west and Capricorn south. All people present are assembled at the zodiac circle, then are asked by a caller to move to their Sun sign, then their Moon sign, Mercury sign, and so on, in unison. Inevitably, they land up in three or four large groups (currently Cancer to Libra) when Pluto is reached, arranged by astrological generation. Then the whole process is unwoven, with everyone moving across the floor from Pluto back through to Sun groups. Ascendants and Midheavens can be included: it's also worth covering Descendants and ICs too. The caller needs to draw people's attention to the patterns which emerge as everyone is mingling and crossing to the next sign. Also, the caller can draw people's attention to their feelings as they move through their chart. 'Horoscope Weaving' is good for a ten-minute warm-up or break between activities, or as a complete awareness exercise, and can be repeated several times, with evolving results.

Medicine Wheel

In Medicine Wheel practice, each direction in a circle is understood to have a specific energy and message, and people sitting there will to some extent be speaking on behalf of that energy. 'Astrological Pow-Wow' is interesting – an astrological mutation of a native American tradition. Here, a Pow-Wow is held in a mandala circle of the zodiac, and people are asked to sit wherever they choose. They do not need to sit in their Sun sign or any deliberately thought-out position: an intuitive or spontaneous place will often prove meaningful, even oracular. A Pow-Wow is then started in the normal way, with people contributing with words, songs or acts of personal meaning, on any theme which arises. Anything is relevant. If the Pow-Wow atmosphere is well-fostered, a pattern will emerge where people are speaking, whether consciously or not, on behalf both of themselves and of the sign, the archetype. It all depends on a certain way of seeing! It is possible to position objects representing each of the planets in their positions as of that day, to amplify the procedure.

In astrological Pow-Wow, every little event is valid: if a bird sings from a certain direction, if there is a gap in the circle, if some are sitting while others are lounging, or if some parts of the circle are emotionally stirred while others are depersonalising and theoretical, all these events say something of revelatory significance.

Here I would like to mention 'Archaeo-astronomical Pow-Wow', invented by dowser-prehistorian Sig Lonegren, a non-astrologer. Neither he nor I have yet had the chance to see this work properly, but we believe it is potent! As usual, people sit in a circle, but there is no fixed zodiac around which people sit. Instead, an awareness is developed and maintained by people present, of the actual physical orientations of the Sun, Moon, planets and signs (or constellations) as seen from the place of the Pow-Wow at that very moment. These positions change gradually (thanks to earth's diurnal rotation) but continually. The people sitting in the direction of each heavenly body (as seen from the centre) are seen to be representing its archetype. Again, it is best that no one deliberately attempts to represent these archetypes, but merely that the connections are noted in the light of all that unfolds in the Pow-Wow. Note, however, that the frame of reference is slowly moving (clockwise): this requires something of an understanding of the dynamics of movement of the heavens, from a 'local space' viewpoint. This technique is probably best practised by prehistory-minded people rather than astrologers – whose astronomical sense can be surprisingly poor! However practised, it could be very potent.

Walking Ephemerides or the Orrery Dance

An 'Orrery Dance' requires a group of reasonably knowledge-able astro-enthusiasts to act out the motions of the planets over a period of time for the others as audience. This reveals some of the beauty of planetary motions and cycles over time. Once I ran such an 'Orrery' to show planetary motions between the Harmonic Convergence (August 1987) and the Uranus–Neptune conjunctions of 1992 – and we sounded a gong whenever a significant 'power point in time' was reached (a full moon, configuration or major aspect).

For this each planet needs to be embodied by a person, furnished with photocopied ephemeris tables for the period concerned. A floor-surface marked with the zodiac is required, plus an 'Ephemeris Person' (representing God?) to check that everyone is moving in harmony with one another, on cue. This person, or another, can also commentate a little, pointing out patterns and configurations, lunar phases and significant aspects for the audience. The representative of the Moon will be pacing the 'Dance' by walking around the circle fastest. This needs rehearsing a few times – and outer planet representatives need the patience to shuffle really slowly! An appropriate time-period is chosen, lasting between two and five years around the present time, perhaps starting and ending on a major configuration. And off it goes!

The thoughts, feelings and experiences of everyone at the time the Dance is being acted out are *all* relevant. It is possible, if the acting astrologers are articulate, for each of them to verbalise or dramatise the planet they are representing, and to show their changes of mood as they interact with other planets.

Another variant of this is to perform a 'Psychodrama of Today', in which a set of people act out the dynamics of today's planetary positions as if it were a birth chart, using the usual psychodrama technique. This can take the emphasis in psychodrama off the personal, and onto the living transpersonal sphere of life.

Turning the Wheel of Time

'Astrological Magic' can take on various forms, but the purpose here is to move into the business of *invoking* the powers (planetary influences or zodiacal principles) which astrology identifies. This is an area of our work which many of today's astrologers appear to forget. Ancient astrologers were shaman-priests, healers, magistrates and channellers as well as being advisers, and were responsible for drawing in positive influences to come to bear on our lives: springtime would not come unless it was *asked* to come. The cycles of world destiny needed invoking: astrologers were (and are?) spiritually committed to 'turning the wheel of time'.

Various means can be used. For example, planet-in-sign subgroups can be set each to create a five-minute invocation of the positive elements of their signs. Or, alternatively, one or several people can get together to design a choreographed rite in which people take roles, representing different astrological principles, with intermittent whole-group involvement in singing, dancing, silence or activity. Or, sign or element groups can be delegated to contribute in certain specific ways: Earth signs by preparing the space; Fire signs by contributing music or drumming, illumination or fire; Air signs by verbalising the rite, incense or motion; and Water signs by providing benediction and refreshments! In all cases, it is good to begin and end the occasion with a Silent Circle, to 'return to centre'. This is an opportunity for everyone to create something – imaginative at minimum, and potentially deeply healing.

The whole procedure needs to have clear and progressive intent, and an instigator needs to make sure that all the relevant stages in the ceremony are fulfilled, and that it is completed with a proper closing and dedication at the end. (The main stages of ceremony are preparation, raising energy, invocation–prayer, enactment–celebration, benediction and receiving blessing, completion, and clearing up.) For me, the purpose of such activities has been to awaken a sense of wonder, to encourage positive attitudes to personal change, and to foster feelings of active participation in world change. Whether it *works* magically, or not, is secondary, for something is gained every time. But there are often strong synchronicities, little demonstrations that something is happening, even if only a change of consciousness: we ended one gathering by singing and attuning on top of Glastonbury Tor (a mysterious and powerful hill), and as we opened our eyes after attuning, a big bright rainbow threw itself across the sky, in that instant! At the end of an invocation to Venus which I once participated in, a setting conjunction of Venus with the waxing crescent moon appeared from behind the clouds, with exact timing and astounding beauty (unexpected by many).

Time in Manifestation

The remarkable thing about any growth-oriented event is that it changes people's consciousness. It takes us out of our everyday concerns and brain-rattlings into another world: time warps and weaves, new meaning and perspectives are seen, and archetypes are demonstrated. An event is succeeding as soon as people start recognising the direct link between the stuff of our psyches and the happenings in our environment – in their own experience.

This is what I call the 'Wish-Fulfilling Karma Exchange' effect. Weird and wonderful connections and synchronicities start happening as the energy rises. People start saying things on each other's behalf, teaching each other and providing solutions for one another. We start representing each other's subpersonalities, or facing each other with things we need to learn – which sometimes can be difficult! But the purpose of these events is not *just* to have a grand time; it is to give each other a gift of awareness and knowledge. If there is assistance at hand in knotty cases, and if there is a consciously guided cycle of energy-changes which leads towards resolution and completion, all difficulties become worthwhile and positive grist to the mill. Everyone goes home feeling enriched and rewarded, empowered to live more fully. As we astrologers say, birth charts show us the potential available to each person: similarly, the astrological array of energy for the present moment has potential, which can be used or overlooked, leading to different outcomes. Gatherings are a good way of working with living astrological energy.

One of the main ideas behind gatherings and camps is to utilise and explore all available forms of learning and education. Additional activities we have had at gatherings have been:

- ordinary talk-workshops by astrologers, to fulfil the advantages of the 'teacher-student' form of education, and focus on specific areas of astrological interest;
- open groups, where, at Pow-Wow, opportunities are given to suggest study groups on specific subjects – here, a group gets together to investigate harmonics, Chiron or current affairs by co-contribution;
- sessions of one-to-ones, co-counselling, or one-astrologer-with-five-clients – to give individuals a chance to gain insight into their own charts, from particular astrologers or others;
- large-group imaging sessions, several psychodrama sessions going on at once (with 12–15 per group), or therapy groups which might not be directly astrological at all;
- trips out to beauty-spots or power-points – this helps in energy-raising or relaxing after intense hours of stimulation, for nature teaches too;
- chanting, music, dancing, storytelling, even written and rehearsed astrological plays (thanks Lindsay River!);
- arranging to dream together during the night, to explore a certain theme;
- extended breaks – the quality of astrology which goes on around café tables can sometimes be exceptional – but it's important also not to let energy dissipate by making these too long;
- spontaneously arising activities – which can sometimes override planned activities, but which if negotiated well with everybody, can lead to improvement of the whole gathering, by leaps and bounds.

143

Astrological Timing

At the astrology camp of 1986, we had an array of Saturn, Mars and Jupiter in the night sky, all 30 degrees apart, with the Moon crossing them during the camp. It became very clear, in direct experience, how astrology had started, thousands of years ago, out in some wilderness, under the light of the Milky Way. I did late-night stargazing workshops, and at the end of them, encouraged people to attune directly to a planet or star, meditatively. Nowadays we use ephemerides rather than astrolabes, but the roots of astrology are calling (at least to some!).

Surely it should be the case that, as far as calendrical and practical considerations allow, astrological (or any) events need to be astrologically timed? For each event I have planned, I have had both diary and ephemeris handy, to juggle practical considerations (weekends, public holidays, and so on), with, moon phase and in a case of fine-tuning what's available (for example, whether to start on Friday evening with the Sun in the 7th or 6th, or Saturday morning with the Sun in the 11th, or waiting until an aspect or ingress has passed).

But on occasions there has been what I call a 'power point in time' to catch. A 'power point in time' is a major astrological 'twang', when several phenomena are happening at once (new or full moons, ingresses, separate or configured aspects, or simply a dense series of independent astro-events). Examples of these are th 'Harmonic Convergence' in August 1987 (very Leonine, and tricky for group events); the 'Halley's Comet weekend', 9 February 1986, when five planets plus the comet were in Aquarius (excellent for groups!); the Saturn–Neptune conjunction, with Jupiter and Chiron opposing, of 13 November 1989 (evidently good for large group gatherings in Leipzig!); or the odd eclipse. The advantage of catching one of these is that it can allow extra chances for a momentous event and for deep energies to come through. The subtle conditions for 'quantum' change are immensely enhanced. (You'll find more information about

144

these matters in my book *Living in Time*.)

While the beginning of any event (and its chart) is important, the sequence of astrological changes throughout, up to the end, are also significant and educative. The main areas of interest are changes of sign on the Ascendant, lunar movements and aspects, ingresses and stations which happen during the event. Some astrological computer programs generate a continually updating on-screen chart for the moment, which can be useful to have running, for anyone to refer to. But it can also be used as an exercise: for example, a prize can be offered to the person who most accurately uses their subtle senses to identify the next change of sign on the Ascendant, out loud, when it happens, without foreknowledge.

I find that the sign position of the Moon is worthy of extra note: if, for example, the event begins with the Moon in Aries or Leo, people find difficulty trusting one another and getting off their pedestals, but it's energetic; if the Moon is in Pisces, timings are difficult to keep, and sometimes enlightening, sometimes chaotically tricky things can arise; if the Moon is in Libra, everyone either follows everyone else around or reacts off them, and if in Gemini they chatter a lot and wander from gaggle to gaggle; in Earth signs, things can sometimes be a bit turgid, but can achieve an intended aim, and in Water signs they can be sometimes deeply sensitised and sometimes self-protective. Each sign has its assets and pitfalls: for gatherings, however, days with Moon in Libra, Sagittarius or Aquarius seem to me to be most conducive.

Similarly, moon phase is important. No one moon phase is better than any other, but it is good to envision your intents in ways which are likely to land up actually fulfilling themselves. Thus, a full moon event will tend to be profound and 'peaky' (or occasionally rather wild or weird), while an old moon event can be contemplative and reflective, or possibly difficult to crank up, or occasionally rich in letting-go-to-the-future possibilities. Half moons tend to be a bit dulling as far as free thinking and playfulness go, but they provide an atmosphere of work or breakthrough which can cover some good growth mileage. Waxing moons can be future-oriented and exploratory, while waning moons can be past-oriented, enriching and reflective. I find it's best to time an exact full or new moon to take place roughly mid-event, to catch the energy, but also to allow time for 'debriefing' afterwards. But I am always prepared to allow for surprises! The issue here is that one cannot predict *what* will happen, but one can get a notion of the energy-parameters within which one can facilitate fruitful developments and outcomes.

Conclusion

Sometimes, it feels to me as if subtle underlying energy *needs* people to channel it and act it out. If an energy finds no easy channel, it will create a convoluted one in order to move from energy-potential to action. In other words, we can either caringly work our way through a Venus–Saturn opposition, or we can walk out on one another and indulge in our aloneness and alienation: the choice is ours. Everything and everyone in this world is interrelated. It is partially with this in mind that I have been moved to instigate these events – if only to offer a focused and spontaneous group energy, through which the Times, the collective unconscious, may speak. I'm a Jupiter in Pisces person, and for me, such a perspective is important! When a largish number of people attune as a circle to a focused resonant energy, spirit speaks with big voice!

When people open up together, they act more from the soul and less from the personality, and have bouts of brilliance which can set developments in motion which reach far further than foreseen. Astrological-archetypal energy expresses itself directly, naturally, and catches on when someone sounds the chord. An example: Moon is conjuncting Pluto in Scorpio, and a succession of people in pow-wow demonstrate that they are 'sitting on their stuff'; then one person chooses suddenly to go into her charged emotions, bursting into tears and muttering about her dead mother; this starts off a chain-reaction of opening up, which may well wander onto other things – but the key has been found, and the energy moves. Moon–Pluto is coming out positively.

These larger gatherings are designed for the moving of energy. It's a kind of initiatory process: it starts off a lot of things for people. Paradoxically, one of the signs of success is that many people don't come back – they're too busy working with what they've found! Although I haven't stressed it in this paper, the gatherings are intellectually and technically very revealing, and the information exchange is tremendous. Would that it could all be recorded, as in a conference! But the point of power is in the present moment: and here, gatherings are useful. They represent one form of *perestroika* in the astrological world, a place of rebirth for our craft, and for all who partake. For me, they have been exciting and challenging (to the extent that I'm taking a rest at the time of writing!), and I'm ready for more, in new places and contexts, and am willing to help others in carefully arranging their own gatherings.

Note

1. Chiron seems to provide what is absolutely appropriate, timely and obvious – even though up to that point it has seemed to be improbable, inconceivable or an obstacle rather than a solution. A person who is a Chiron manifestation suggests or acts out what everyone needs, though often initially seeming to be an uncomfortable or strange presence, or a thorn in everyone's side. Usually, such a person is the least likely person to bring what they bring.

=== 8 ===

SOLAR QUEST

Lindsay River

Commentary

From detailed theory we return to practical experience.
Lindsay River maps out an imaginative journey, a quest for
the Self which anyone can follow. The exercise is designed
to bring out our conscious self-determination (the Sun)
rather than the lunar reactiveness which tells us so much
about our unconscious assumptions, and for this reason it
is presented not as a guided fantasy led by a facilitator,
but as an exercise in creative writing. This will be a new
experience for many people, for it is neither the Saturnian task
of accurately reporting objective information, nor the lunar
experience of observing the products of personal fantasy,
but the solar activity of consciously shaping material which
is spontaneously given by the imagination. Just as in psychodrama, the writer is at liberty to experiment, intervene and
otherwise mould the products of inner fantasy. In the same
way, according to astrological symbolism, we shape and
determine the course of our lives through our solar identity,
which is able to work creatively on the material given by
'Fate', or its own nature and the remainder of the horoscope.
Lindsay gives detailed instructions for making this journey,
followed by the tales of some travellers who have already been
there.

P. H. J.

This is the story of a quest.[1] It will be your own quest, for your own self, because it is knowledge of the self that is attained at the end of all journeys.

As astrologers we know that the Sun represents the Self, our capability to integrate the various, often conflicting, parts of our being, our ability to say 'I am', to define our own identity. It is not surprising that the Sun in the horoscope tells us much about our health and potential to recover from setbacks – it is this acceptance and integration of the many parts of our natures (astrologically, the planets) and this power of self-definition that are the major keys to recovery and health.

It is the solar quest that we shall undertake, the search of the Self for itself that is paralleled by the Sun's journey through the zodiac each year. Each of us will start at a different point in the zodiac, at the degree of the Sun on our birthdate, because each person's quest is individual. Yet our own personal quests draw strength from their resonance with myths and legends of the Sun's adventures through the zodiac.

When humankind first watched the skies they seem to have originally discovered the phases and movements of the Moon, and the pattern of the constellations whose rising and setting at certain times of the night foretold the seasons' changes. Later they perceived the motions of the planets through the zodiac. In Mesopotamia the planets were named 'wild goats', in Greece 'wanderers' to emphasise their nomadic, journeying nature. It was still later in the history of skywatching (probably in the second millennium BCE) that it was realised that the Sun, too, appears to move through the zodiac from the perspective of the earth-dweller. Around that time myths began to be told of the solar hero who travelled through different lands or faced different trials. Heracles' labours and Samson's conquest of the lion (Leo) and defeat at the hands of Delilah (*Dly* in Hebrew, the same word as is used for the sign Aquarius[2]) have been interpreted as solar myths.

The journey of the solar hero around the zodiac each year may have combined with the exploits of historical traveller heroes to inspire the many legends of the brave individual

149

who encounters guides, enemies and numerous wonders in an allegorical journey through life. The journeying hero is most often depicted as male (Gilgamesh in the Sumerian epic, Odysseus, Everyman, Tripitaka in the Chinese Buddhist classic *Journey to the West*, Maelduin in the Irish Gaelic epic, knightly questers for the Holy Grail, Christian in *Pilgrim's Progress*, Sinbad in *The Arabian Knights*). Yet some of the early seekers and questers were female (Ishtar on her quest for Dumuzi in the Underworld, Isis searching for the dismembered body of Osiris, Demeter seeking Persephone). Folk-tale has given us female questers such as Gerda in *The Snow Queen* and many other brave female heroes of traditional tales. Though Isis is usually a lunar rather than a solar figure, the dismembered Osiris may in fact represent the Moon (which has pieces 'cut off' as it wanes each month). The unhesitating modern description of the Sun as masculine and the Moon as feminine is not paralleled in ancient tradition, where solar goddesses abound in many cultures.

The Horoscope as Landscape

To discover your own astrological landscape for your solar quest you will need to know astrological basics (the meanings of planets, signs and houses) and to have your chart calculated and drawn up. The details will be fuller if you know your time of birth, and hence the house cusps in your horoscope, but you can also undertake your solar quest with a chart that has been drawn up for noon at your birthdate, and without the house cusps marked in – planets in signs only being shown. Possession of an accurate horoscope with an exact time of birth is a great privilege, and it is important that voyages of self-discovery do not exclude those without this advantage.

Your journey will begin at the position of the Sun in your horoscope. On your birthday (or the day before or after it) the transiting Sun reaches this same point in the horoscope each year. In the following months the Sun will move around

150

your horoscope and pass by (or conjunct) each planet and the cusps of signs and/or houses in their turn. This sequence of astrological events provides the adventures on your solar quest. The journey you will imaginatively create can give you images that may help you to understand better your own inner landscape and its denizens, and your annual quest for self-knowledge.

This is a *solar* quest, not a lunar one, for it is the annual passage of the Sun through the horoscope that is described. You will need to call on your lunar faculties of imagination to create the landscape and its inhabitants, yet develop your solar qualities as you proceed on your quest. The exercise that follows is designed to emphasise the solar attributes of conscious choice, chosen self-expression and the expression of the identity through the will. You will find that you are constantly being asked to exercise your solar faculties by making conscious choices. While the lunar world of the imagination calls us to explore deeply in the unconscious, the solar path requires us to define for our conscious Selves how much we are ready to discover.

Creative Writing as a Medium of Self-discovery

The exercise is designed so that you may write your own journey, at your own pace, and in your own way. There are advantages in the use of creative writing as compared to other methods of self-discovery that I have used in workshop situations and with individuals. Guided fantasy *could* be used for this solar journey, but there can be problems in allowing people to work at their own pace. Some people will find they are being asked to deal with too much of their charts too quickly. Our charts vary so much that a densely packed area of discovery for one person could coincide with a much simpler part of the journey for another participant. Even if the facilitator guides the fantasy at an average pace it will be too fast for some people, while a very slow pace will send others to sleep.

151

In favour of creative writing rather than guided meditation or fantasy is the way unconscious material (which may be disturbing if it emerges too fast) can be selected by the conscious mind in the writing process. The level at which we engage with our inner selves can be determined with more sense of control.

Working too fast can lead to psychological indigestion – too much material from the unconscious being dragged up with too little time to integrate it. It is important in this exercise to work at the right pace – stay with one area of your chart until you feel that you have finished with it (for the moment – you can always return). It is also important to let the right amount of time elapse between sessions within your astrological landscape, so that you can bring what you have learned into your everyday life and experience. This way, working with your chart becomes a tool for living your life rather than an escape from it. Those with Uranus square Neptune (mid 1950s) may have to be particularly wary of allowing astrology to become a retreat from life.

I would suggest you do not try to write more than one house or sign of your journey in a week. One house or sign per month would be appropriate to the time-scale of the Sun, which transits one sign in a month. If you have some areas of your chart which are packed with planets, or one house or sign which is very difficult for you, you might want to take much longer to work on it. It would not be too surprising if a meeting with Pluto took two years to write about – we take as long or longer to get to grips with our Pluto transits!

It is also perfectly in order to pass through a difficult area of your chart without encountering any planet situated there, or to breeze quickly through a tricky house without noticing much of the landscape. It is your horoscope, and your exercise. You can come back later when the time is right for you to approach this area or planet again, just as the Sun returns annually to the 'trouble spots' in our charts, giving us multiple chances to understand them better.

When you choose your own timing it allows you to be in charge – *you* know best what you need. Honour your intuition about yourself and never feel you *ought* to complete a section in detail. There are no 'oughts' in this exercise, though there are suggestions as to how best to conduct your quest.

Taking Responsibility for Yourself

Honour the signs, houses and planets you encounter on your quest – they are all parts of yourself. Even if, for instance, you have many problems with Pisces and you imagine that the Pisces section will be a very alien landscape within your horoscope, remember that Pisces is a part of yourself that you are attempting to know better. We all have every one of the signs within us, although some are far more developed than others.

Show respect for the planets in your writing. It would not be a good idea, for instance, to give Saturn (which you have just described as a huge leaden statue blocking your way) an almighty whack with a stick just because you are fed up with your Saturn return. By writing like this you would be insulting your own Saturn energy, your desire for responsibility, your appetite for self-discipline, consolidation, stability. (And in any case, you would probably break the stick . . .)

If you know that the matters associated with a certain sign, house or planet are particularly loaded for you, this might not be the right time to write about them in detail. It is probably wiser to acknowledge Mars and pass on if you are feeling terrified of your anger, rather than writing an encounter with the planet.

What can you do if your imagination surprises you and you feel quite upset by something you have written? If you are not sure how to integrate your self-discovery it can be useful to find some help. Talking with other astrologers, or with friends who can understand the emotions you are describing (if not the astrological symbolism) can be helpful. You may want to see an astrological counsellor if there is one accessible to you, or a counsellor or therapist who could help you to address the emotional issues even if the astrology means little to them. If this kind of help is not what you want, or if you cannot afford or find it, then there are various methods of self-help you might consider. Reading well-written astrology books that cover the planet, sign or house that is proving tricky for you may be a good method. Another which may work as well, or better, could be to leave astrological interpretation alone and see how your everyday experience and conversations with friends can bring you illumination on the issues that trouble you.

One Quester's Map

Figure 13 shows Anna's horoscope. Her quest begins in Taurus in the 7th house, for this is the position of her Sun. She need not start this journey of creative writing on or near her birthday, but she will begin to describe her own landscape from this place in her chart. Firstly she will describe (in as much detail as is appropriate for her) what she herself is wearing and the environment in which she finds herself (a Taurean 7th house). She may or may not describe a Mercury figure (Mercury is conjunct the Sun and hence close to the solar quester) as she wishes. She is, in any case, leaving Mercury behind and moving towards the end of her 7th house. She will go on to describe how her environment changes as she enters Gemini and the 8th house, and tell about her encounter with the Moon, if she is ready for this experience. The journey ahead of her stretches through a Geminian 8th house and moves through the Cancerian 9th and past the planet Uranus. Her quest moves on towards the Midheaven in Leo, the planet Pluto, and the following signs and planets in their order, until she crosses the Ascendant and eventually, after traversing the lower half of her chart, comes round again to the position she started from, the place of the Sun at 26 degrees Taurus.

Anna's chart has its house cusps and sign cusps very close

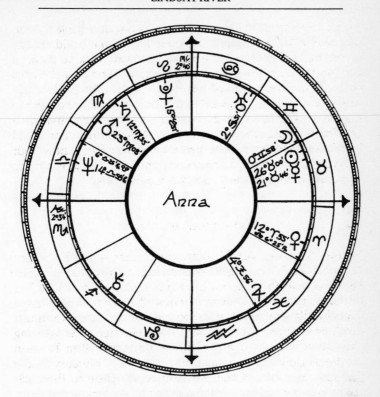

Fig. 13   Anna's birth chart (birth data withheld for confidentiality)

together. In her journey she finds that the landscape changes its nature quite definitely from house to house, because the sign changes at the same time, or nearly so. For another quester who has the house cusps in the middle of signs, or two signs in one house, the changes of environment would not be so sudden. For instance, in a very different chart to Anna's the quester writes about a bank in a foreign country (his image for a Sagittarius 2nd house, the place of his Sun). The Sagittarian atmosphere remains as the quester moves on to describe the

155

3rd house (still within Sagittarius) and finds himself in a school opposite the bank where he is being taught in a language he has never heard before, but which, miraculously, he understands. As he moves on towards Capricorn (still in the 3rd house) he goes to the vacant headmaster's office in this school.

All the examples I quote here are merely individual responses to the concepts of Sagittarius, Capricorn and 2nd and 3rd houses. Another person might envisage a similar combination of signs and houses quite differently – her whole chart might be described as outdoor landscapes with no urban buildings, it might include sea, caves, mountains, deserts or outer space. It could even be contained within one mansion with twelve rooms, depending on the imaginative choices of the quester.

Your Resources

When you start your quest in the house and sign of your Sun, you find with you a bag containing eleven gifts (ten if Chiron is not marked into your chart). These gifts are not visible to you at the beginning of your journey, being contained within the bag, and you do not examine them at this stage. Ten (or nine without Chiron) of these are for the planetary beings you will pass by or encounter on your journey. The eleventh is a gift for yourself (the Sun) when you return again to your starting-point. The bag has magical properties so that the gift may be as large or as small as you wish once it has emerged from the bag. When you pass by or encounter a planetary being you will discover what the gift actually is by describing what you take out of the bag.

Your Solar Quest

Prepare

Find writing materials and a quiet and comfortable place to write about your quest. You may like to work together with a friend, comparing each stage of your respective journeys on completion of a section.

The exercise is designed to be undertaken as **creative writing** (though it could be spoken into a tape recorder). It would be constructed differently if it were a guided fantasy, and will probably not work well if you turn it into one. If you are working together with a friend you should make a copy of these instructions for each of you.

Have your horoscope in front of you. You will need to refer to it to chart your journey. If you are not a seasoned astrologer, you may need to have a good astrological textbook by you, so that you can consult it to find helpful keywords for signs, houses and planets that may help to stimulate your imagination and allow you to write about your journey. Above all, this exercise is not an exam or a memory test!

Beginning your quest

Your Sun is in . . . sign and in the . . . house (supply the details for yourself, including the house if you know your time of birth. If you do not, ignore the following directions that refer to houses).

You, the quester, find yourself in an environment appropriate to the sign and house above.

Write down a description of the environment around you. Is it indoors? Outdoors? What sort of furnishings? Landscape? What are you doing in the sign/house? (If you know your time of birth and have the houses drawn into your chart you will be describing an environment that is created by both sign *and* house.) Examine the clothing that you, the quester, are wearing. What is the bag like that you have with you, full of gifts for the planets?

As you write your answers to these questions, be aware that you can change your mind about any detail that you are not happy with. Go into as much or as little detail as you wish, depending on how comfortable you feel with this

157

house and/or sign, or how intrepid an explorer you wish to be.

If a certain area such as 'family' or 'partnership' is very emotionally loaded for you, you can choose to write about Cancer and the 4th house or Libra and the 7th house in more general ways – describing an ideally safe place for Cancer/4th house, for instance, or creating your preferred environment in which to meet a close personal friend for Libra/7th house. Remember that all the signs and houses have many meanings and associations – you can choose what you like best or what is most appropriate for you at this time.

If your sun is on the cusp of a sign or a house you may be able to envisage two different environments, one behind you and one ahead of you. How do they contrast? Have they anything in common? (Someone born with the Sun on the Capricorn/Aquarius cusp and in the middle of the 6th house might describe two landscapes, one Capricornian and one Aquarian. Yet the landscapes will have something in common because they both have a 6th house quality. There are also often surprising similarities between adjacent signs.)

If you feel stuck, refer to the keywords you remember or can consult in your astrology book – what sort of environment do they suggest for your Sun, for the beginning of your quest?

After you have written down some description, note down your feelings and reflections about the environment you are describing. Perhaps you are gaining greater insights about the sign or house in question – be sure to note down anything you realise now, but had never realised before.

If you are not happy with something you describe, remember, *you are the creator* – change it. If you write a cave, but don't want to write yourself going into it, you can scrap the image, or write yourself a path that goes round the cave.

Once you have created an environment around you, consider:

Is/Are there (a) planet(s) in the sign/house through which you are journeying? As you approach the planet (or the first of the planets proceeding anticlockwise round your chart from the place of your Sun) at the beginning/middle/end of the sign/house,

Ask yourself

Do I want to write an encounter with this planet or only to leave a gift and pass on?

If you want to pass on without an encounter,

Write down what you find in your magical bag as a gift for the planet. Describe the gift as fully as you want to. Where do you want to leave it as an offering – choose the right place in the environment you have created for the sign/house.

If you want to write an encounter with the planet,

Ask yourself

Would I like my encounter with this planet to be distant? Closer?

If distant, write down what the planetary being looks like to you. Is it a person? An animal? A bird? A symbolic object? Something else? How far away from you is this being? You may wish to write about a quick glimpse, or a fuller vision.

Describe the being as fully or briefly as you would like – pay attention to colours, shape, garments, atmosphere, expression. If it is a person or an animal, is it female? Male? Both? Neither? Is its sex unclear? Irrelevant? Is it young? Old?

What does this being seem to be doing in the environment you have created for this sign/house?

When you have finished describing the planetary being, *write down* your thanks to it for revealing itself to you and pass on through the sign/house, unless you wish for a closer encounter.

If you would like a closer encounter with the planetary being, complete all the descriptions under the distant encounter above, then,

Ask yourself

Do I have anything I want to ask this being? Is there anything this being wants me to know?

Write down any conversation you have, any message given to you.

159

When your writing of the interaction between yourself as quester and the planetary being seems to be completed and you have written it into being as you wish to,
Write down your thanks to the planetary being for communicating with you.

If you have planets conjunct to each other in this sign/house (aspects other than the conjunction are ignored in this exercise) you may wish to discover how the planets relate to each other. If so, **write down** any interaction you see between the planets. Does one seem stronger or more attractive to you? Is one easier to describe? Do they seem to work together well or with difficulty? Does one seem to be more at ease in the environment you have created for this sign/house? Are they conjunct, but across sign or house cusps? How do you imagine that this affects their interaction?

When you have completed any description of the planets' interaction,
write down your thanks to the planets for revealing more of their relationship with each other.

When you are feeling complete with the planet(s) you have encountered,
write down what you find in your magical bag as a gift for these planetary being(s). Describe your gift(s) as fully as you want to. Do you hand the gift to the planet? Leave it on the ground? Place it somewhere in particular? If you wish to you can describe how the planet reacts to the gift.

Finally write down anything else you need to say about this sign/house. Consider whether the journey through this sign/house that you have written has been a development for you. Are you more at ease within the environment than when you first entered it? Have you gained any insights from your passing through this part of your horoscope?

Decide whether you are going to stop writing at the next sign cusp or the next house cusp, or before then. (You can stop at any time.)

When you have completed all the description you need at this time for the sign/house and any of its inhabitants in the environment you have created
Draw a line under your writing.

Look around the space you are sitting in and remember what you were doing before you started this exercise, what you intended to do after finishing it. This is an important part of the process so that you can 'close off' from the imaginary world of your writing and reconnect with your everyday life.

Give yourself some appreciation for being a brave and creative person. Do this especially if you avoided encounters, got 'stuck' in the exercise, or couldn't think/feel what to put down.

Reread what you have written if you wish to. Then,
Write down
Any feelings you have now.
Anything that this exercise has told you about yourself and your horoscope.
Any particular relevance that this part of your journey has to your life at the moment or your experience in the past.

How can you use what you have learned about yourself and this part of your horoscope creatively in your life?

When you have completed these notes,
Draw another line and reconnect with the room, your everyday life in a fuller way. Decide what you want to do now. (This may be different from what you planned to do, and if you do not have pressing responsibilities you may be able to change your plans.)

When you are ready to create more of your solar quest after an intervening lapse of time/'real life' you can start again at the beginning of this exercise and work with the next section of your chart.

Note down now the point in your chart (degree of the zodiac or particular house or sign cusp) where you finished today. This will provide you with your starting-point next time.

Be careful not to gallop through your horoscope at breakneck speed. You need a chance to digest each part of your solar quest and integrate it into your life.

Your Solar Quest as a Whole

You may, over time, complete your whole horoscope and reach the place you started from, the position of your Sun. This would be a good time to reread your solar quest to see how much you have changed since you wrote the first sequence – or you may like to read the 'journey so far' every time you complete one section. When you have given the last gift to the Sun (your Self) you will find a new bag of gifts to give the planets waiting for you. It is worth describing your Self (the Sun) as you now see her. As you become aware of the way that she has grown and changed you can start to describe the house she is in as she would see it. It may look very different from the way it did the last time round. When you look from her perspective you will merge into a new sense of Self, and realise your achievements in integrating the growth and change in your solar journey.

If you wish, you can start to undertake your solar quest again, making deeper (or perhaps, lighter) interactions with the planets and the environment of sign and house in which they are discovered.

Once you are familiar with your own changing landscape you can also use it as a basis for other exercises in creative writing. You might decide to write your solar quest again month by month, starting at your birthday (if you did not do this before) and keeping pace with the Sun in its apparent movement around the zodiac. For instance, as the Sun reaches

0 degrees Libra at the Equinox you would write about the environment at 0 degrees Libra in your own chart. By doing this you will create simultaneous images for the transit of your horoscope by the Sun. Writing sessions could be scheduled for the actual days that the Sun transits the planet or house cusp in question. This project would take some discipline (and flexibility in your life) to maintain, but it would be very interesting to see if greater insights came to you while you were under the influence of an actual transit.

You could also use the landscape discovered on your solar quest as a medium to explore the meanings for you of other transiting planets. For instance, if Pluto has just entered your 11th house you could consult your notes on your solar quest to read your description of the 11th house. Discovering that your 11th house was (for instance) a vast conference centre where all your friends and others with similar interests were discussing sexuality, death, and the possibility of an afterlife (Scorpio 11th house) you could now write a sequence in which Pluto comes into the main conference hall. How would people react to Pluto? What would Pluto have to say, and how might your friendships and interests be transformed by this new visitor? This exercise might be a fruitful one to help you prepare yourself for Pluto's transit of the house.

Of course, transits never quite turn out as we expect them to! The contrast between what we imagine beforehand and our later reflections is itself an important mode of self-discovery. It can be worth keeping the notes you write about your transits to discover this contrast later, and so construct your astrological autobiography. Whatever you choose to do with your solar quest, congratulate yourself as a resourceful traveller, the hero of your own life.

Travellers' Tales

Your imagery for signs, houses and planets is unique, coming from your own imagination. You may prefer not to hear accounts from other wayfarers in case these influence you and affect too strongly what you create for yourself. Most of us only borrow images from others when they resonate for us, however many stories from fellow questers we listen to. If you would like to you could draw nearer to the fire and listen to the tales of others on their solar quests.

My own journey began in a Geminian 12th house (the house of my Sun) where I wandered, self-absorbed, in a tower filled with books until I encountered a scholarly and eccentric character amongst the book stacks. Uranus' advice to me was on the lines of 'To your own self be true' and fortified me for the journey across my Cancer Ascendant (which involved a descent into the lower part of my chart through a sea-cave).

Anna (whose horoscope is shown in Figure 13) found herself in a solid and affluent (Taurean) mansion in which the inhabitants related to each other in traditional ways (Taurus 7th house). She felt like a secluded princess, or the Sleeping Beauty who was trapped in the mansion. Each of her relationships with the house happened privately, on a one-to-one basis, so that she could gain no wider perspective on these interactions. When she tried to discover her own identity (her Sun) all that seemed to be available was to accept a part of the mansion's identity for herself. The grandeur and plenty around her seemed stultifying and rigid. She resolved to leave.

Outside the gate of the mansion (the cusp of her 8th house) she met the Moon (a woman dressed in shimmering silvery rainbow robes, 'who felt rather than looked big'). Anna put her hand in her bag to discover what gift she was carrying for her Gemini Moon. As she pulled out a jewelled star brooch she realised she had brought it with her from the mansion because its resale value would surely help her on her journey. (Note that the 8th house which she is entering is the house of inheritance.) She hardly hesitated a moment, and paid her tribute to the Moon. Her deeper learning began then (Gemini 8th house) as she faced what was unknown and frightening in the landscape beyond.

164

Barbara began her quest at a carnival site where she danced her Leonine, 5th house joy in being alive amidst scenes of exhilaration and creativity. Her dance took her towards a neat and orderly corner of the site where she found a healing space organised under canvas. (She was still within her 5th house but had crossed the cusp from Leo to Virgo.) While most of the people within this healing area were quiet and unobtrusive she came across a disruptive character very much at odds with the general atmosphere. He was pulling out the tent pegs and running away laughing as the structures collapsed on those inside. Once Barbara had met with her Uranus in Virgo she came to understand the 'efficiency' and healing power of disruptive fun. Her gift to Uranus was a pair of scissors, to enable him to cut the tent strings.

By finding these scissors in her magical bag Barbara enacted Uranus' advice to her, which was 'Surprise yourself and do something original!' Before she had written her account of the meeting with this planetary being she might well have imagined a less radical and unusual gift for him. This is one of the reasons why the magical bag that the quester carries does not reveal its contents until the moment the gift is due to manifest.

Her meeting with Uranus prepared Barbara for the more devastating and yet necessary teachings that Pluto had for her. He saw a storm approaching that would totally lay waste the area, 'so that the real healing could begin'. Barbara honoured Pluto's teachings and gave him his gift. She was then ready to meet a woman who came from the tent behind Pluto. This was Barbara's Venus in Virgo, who held Pluto around the waist and kissed his neck. Together the two planetary beings manifested their conjunction as the healing power of sexual love. Barbara gave Venus a red rose in thanks before continuing on her journey.

Barbara had found a dark crystal ball to give to Pluto – his potentially terrifying message about the need to destroy the familiar was made acceptable and harmonious for her (perhaps because she has Venus conjunct Pluto in her chart) and her gift reflected this in its beauty. Other questers' gifts to Pluto have included (from someone with Pluto conjunct responsible Saturn) a journal inscribed 'The Whole Truth', from another a piece of volcanic rock, and, from someone who met a ravening Pluto in Cancer, the most awe-inspiring of the gifts – a piece of raw meat which she threw to him.

Questers have met Mercury as a golden child, as a sea sprite, an elf, as messenger to the gods or as the wielder of the healing caduceus. They have met Mars as warrior, as master of martial arts, as the driver of a racing car (in Aries) or a steamroller (in Taurus). You may find that Mars looks like the woman who teaches your evening class on self-assertion, or that the planet passes through the sign so fast that you cannot discern any features.

Whatever the details of your quest, and however many or few planetary beings you choose to encounter distantly or more closely, your story will be uniquely detailed and capable of continuing development – in fact, just like your horoscope.

Notes

1. The author is adapting this exercise to a role-playing adventure game for computer, and reserves all rights over such or similar adaptation.
2. *The Astrological Secrets of the Hebrew Sages* (Inner Traditions International, New York), by Rabbi Joel C. Dobin, 1977.

GROUP INVOLVEMENT AND CREATIVE ASTROLOGY

Suffolk Astrological Society
(Tina Cox and Glenda Cole)

Commentary

This collection ends with a piece from one of the many local astrology groups which keep astrology alive in Britain. The Suffolk Astrological Society has been exploring creative techniques for several years, and here they describe some of their experiences, together with useful guidelines for any peer group using these methods without a facilitator to guide the action. These guidelines, which centre on the provision of trust and respect, will also be helpful for individuals using creative techniques. We have to trust our own greater Self, its urge to growth as well as its resistances, and respect ourselves and others as unique and important human beings. The Suffolk astrologers stress the need for this vision, and go on to report some of the many breakthroughs in astrological understanding and personal expression which they have made using Creative Astrology techniques. Their success points the way for non-specialists generally who may want to integrate creative exploration of whatever sort with the responsibilities of ordinary adult life.

P. H. J.

Having helped to found and develop the Suffolk Astrological Society over the last ten years, we have learnt to welcome and trust new discoveries in this group environment. Many joint insights and collective lessons have been brought to light by sharing with friends within the group. Fresh ideas and new perspectives are always welcome as this helps keep the stimulation flowing. Creative Astrology is just one of the ideas that has grown in this way; we have found that this method of working not only enhances group involvement but also creates new meaning and insight into astrological symbolism. It is also an excellent way of recognising the creativity, potential and self-expression of ourselves as individuals.

Our method of working with Creative Astrology grew from us experimenting together after having attended various workshops and seminars. Further ideas grew from reading books on subjects other than astrology which contained ideas that we felt could be adapted into creative ways of working with a symbolic language such as astrology. To focus on and put these ideas into practice, we decided it was time to introduce our group to some of them via our regular discussion evenings. Here we looked at different ways to explore the meanings of the planets in our charts, so we asked our members to bring along an object that to them represented either Venus or Mars. The idea was to explore the meanings of these personal symbols with relevance to the chart position and aspects of each planet. On the evening in question those present divided into two smaller groups; one to explore Mars objects and the other Venus. The relevance of each object was discussed, along with the feelings that lay behind each particular choice. Many insights were gained that night and we were to follow the idea through to conclusion on the next discussion evening when we had a complete reversal of roles; wherein the initial Venus group brought along Mars objects to explore and the original Mars group went on to explore Venus objects. We then looked at the relationship of the two symbols/planets within each person's chart.

One woman brought a piece of fool's gold to represent her Mars in Scorpio. This had been an instinctive choice, as were all the objects that were chosen that night, and the only reason she could think of was that she did not know how this Mars manifested in her life. She felt it was foolish to have such a strongly placed planet and not know how it worked. On the following evening her symbol for 3rd house Venus was a pen. Communicating and writing were things she valued above all. When someone asked her if she had written anything the answer she gave was 'Nothing yet!' At this point the woman made the connection between her fool's gold and the pen. She had not yet given her pen any direction by putting energy into her writing. To have an idea and not to use it, she thought, was indeed a very foolish thing. Astrological connections were made with regard to this when it was realised that her Mars was stationary and in an almost exact sesiquadrate to Venus. As a result of this exercise she decided it was time to put her creative talent into action by writing with a view to publication. This self-exploration by chosen objects had helped the woman to realise that Mars needn't be a stationary and an unknown factor in her life. Opening up to this idea she began to use it in making more positive steps forward.

This exercise helped people to discover whether active, masculine Mars, or creative, feminine Venus was stronger within their experience. This was discovered when it came across quite strongly that some people felt more comfortable in the Venus group and others preferred to be in the Mars group. The personal interaction between the two planets was also immensely significant to some, as it brought to light the recognition of which planet was dominant. It could be seen by looking at the relationship of the two together how the underplayed factor could be used more positively without losing or repressing either of the two sets of energies. This initial foray into Creative Astrology seemed to take off very well. The energy stimulated by this particular theme evoked such interest in the group that even after the meetings had finished the topic was still under discussion.

We have also looked at Jupiter and Saturn in this way. It was interesting to note that the the symbols for Jupiter bore a marked similarity in that many were books. However, the content of each book said a lot about the type of knowledge individual people valued. For a Taurean Jupiter it was a gardening book, while for a 9th house Jupiter it was a philosophy book. Another common theme for Jupiter seemed to be one of trust. The ideas developed during this discussion were the fact that some people can be too trusting, whereas others may need to trust a little more. Sharing in these concepts helped us to see both the values and the pitfalls in these different experiences of trust. One person brought along a gnome as her object, but because she had selected this purely instinctively, she had no idea why she had attributed it to Jupiter. As she began speaking she realised it was because she valued and trusted in things that were not necessarily of the material world. She discovered that her concept of learning and knowing was of considerable importance to her and her way of accepting her own Sagittarian Jupiter.

Some Saturn objects depicted were: a clock, from a Capricorn Sun with Virgo rising who ran his life to a strict timetable; household bills from the woman with Saturn in difficult aspect to her 2nd house Jupiter, who felt the material responsibilities of Saturn weighed heavily; and even a boomerang from someone with Saturn square 9th house Neptune who felt that the karmic aspect of Saturn was very much like a boomerang in that 'it would come back to you'. Each of these themes was explored in considerable detail and hopefully each person went home with some new and fresh insights to explore. One particular Saturn group was sprinkled with outbursts of laughter, which led us on to explore humour as a relief to sadness or depression. On the same night the Jupiter group appeared to be very serious as they explored the more philosophical and deeper aspects of the planet. It was quite a surprise to see this in operation as the immediate expectation would have been the jovial Jupiter group and the sombre Saturn group. This proved to us that Creative

Astrology reveals unexpected treasures in understanding the hidden aspects of our astrological expectations.

Enthused by the success of our self-experimentation and of our group's discussions we asked our members if they would like to participate in an experimental, Creative Astrology Workshop. We felt Creative Astrology could offer marvellous insights for both the newcomer and the experienced astrologer alike. By participating in this particular form of astrology we are discovering more than we could if learning and memorising the general meanings of signs, houses and aspects from textbooks. Such books take a lot of reading and understanding and can only take you so far in getting immediately in touch with your own birth chart. By seeing and observing Creative Astrology in action we are learning to actually 'live' our chart energies within ourselves and this is a far more direct approach in the understanding of what astrological symbolism means to each individual; this in turn can lead to far deeper insights, as in this way astrology becomes alive and those involved can discover an inner, personal understanding through their own experiences as a unique individual. Our original suggestion sparked enough interest for us to go ahead with a workshop for our group and from that first experience we decided to develop further skills and ideas in order to bring future workshops to fruition, for those whose interest had already been stimulated.

One advantage of workshop participants belonging to a local group such as ours is that everyone knows each other, even if only as a face seen a few times. This element of familiarity is a good basis on which trust and sharing can be built. Our astrological involvement with a group of such long standing led us to feel that we had a very good grounding for working with astrology on an inspirational level, especially as we had already maintained a good degree of trust and friendliness within the group – something that is of considerable importance when working in this way. In fact we have discovered that Creative Astrology does even more to help the group enhance these very qualities. As part of

171

a group, we are used to sharing astrological knowledge and experience, covering as many fields as possible within the astrological world. A willingness to listen with an open mind is an essential quality when working with people on an individual level – one of the reasons why we think our workshops have been so successful.

We see the workshops as a collective experience and as such no one person leads the group. Consequently the awareness and understanding that is already a vital part of our group remains alive; this togetherness might be somewhat lost if we invited an outside facilitator who was unfamiliar to the group. The general feeling is that as a group we are all learning together and those that attend feel that each person's experience of astrology, and of life itself, is a very good way to encounter one's self-enlightenment in a caring and trusting manner.

We feel that astrological interpretations are in one sense collective and in another individual. Thousands of years of observation have given us collective meanings for the signs, planets and the various aspects within a natal chart; and yet a natal chart also represents an individual and as such interpretation should be coloured by that particular individual's view of reality. The interpretation of Sun conjunct Mars, for instance, can be explored on an inner level by the individual with this particular aspect. In this way a personal understanding of the collective view, which is that Sun conjunct Mars indicates drive, energy and restlessness, formulates into a personal experience for the individual concerned.

Surprisingly we are more aware than we think in our understanding of where another person is coming from and we can often perceive on an instinctive level another person's unconscious processes. It is not really a question of being right or wrong but rather one of trusting those perceptions in regard to the person, or the chart in question, at that particular moment in time. Through experience we have discovered that the things expressed are usually entirely relevant to the situation. Sometimes we have found that at the start of the day the people involved are often worried about their ability to trust in their own intuition, but as the day progresses this is usually forgotten, especially as things have a habit of developing on exactly the lines that they should; this in turn encourages creative self-expression in all of the people involved in the day's exploration, whatever part they may play. When we step out of our own world for a moment we can share with another the various difficulties and struggles that they are likely to encounter during their lives, and again share their discovery of how these situations can be understood and perhaps turned to personal advantage. Thus we learn valuable lessons in acceptance. It is sometimes the shared experience that carries the biggest impact and small groups working together in this new and different way can achieve tremendous results in understanding how basic planetary energies are working or not working for the individual in question.

Our workshops are constantly evolving and changing as we and our group learn from them. Although we use various methods of astrological creativity the main basis of our workshops tends to revolve around role-play wherein participants act out the role of astrological planets, signs or aspects. During such role-play participants are asked not to speak and act as themselves, but as the astrological character they have been assigned to. By playing this type of subjective role people find that it often reveals a formerly hidden awareness. It's rather like getting a group of actors together and deciding on what play you are going to start with. Having thus decided, various people within the group will be cast in a certain role, usually decided by the person who has offered the chart on which to base the play. It may start off with a major aspect pattern depicted in the chart, perhaps a T-square. In this case three actors will be assigned the role of the planets they will be playing. Two actors can interact as the two opposing planets and another can enact the third squaring planet.

When involved in this particular exercise, it has been our experience that the situation can appear to reach a stalemate, as is likely if you are working on a fixed T-square; it may be that players are getting out of hand with their dialogue or are just going round in circles without any positive conclusion being reached. At this point it can often be quite rewarding for a person to view their particular role-play from a new angle or different perspective, as this can offer an alternative way of approaching or working with the dynamics involved. With this objective in mind we decided it would be a good idea to cast a further person in the role of director. Basically the director's job is to be an observer (as indeed is that of the others in the group). It will be the director's job to make suggestions, change the scene around, or ask the actors if they feel that they can reach any sort of compromise. This type of intervention can change the whole scenario of the play. We have found that by casting a director the interactions that take place seem to develop and lead on to a far more positive conclusion. The director as such, does not take charge of the actors but steps in after a certain period of time has elapsed only in order to make suggestions to the players. It is important that all participants, including the director, have the ability to listen and encourage both the positive and negative aspects of any situation or configuration that they are exploring at the time. It may appear to the observer that things seem to be taking a negative stance but it is important to let the play develop fully of its own accord as the actors can often reach their own conclusion without the intervention of a director. It is not a question of the director telling the individuals involved how to deal with their particular themes, but rather to help and encourage them to explore their inner world from a different angle. As has been mentioned, the rest of the group who have not been allocated roles are asked to become observers of the dynamics being enacted. No one judges the rights or wrongs of the role-players, the director or the observers, as the workshop is purely intuitive. After the play has reached its completion, which often happens of its own accord when participants have explored the dynamics to the full, all of the people concerned can then discuss what has taken place. Therefore the observer's role is just as important as that of the participants who take an active role, for through such discussion each person's subjective view of the play can bring forth different insights. In fact the understanding of another's point of view that has been gained by becoming involved tends to make one forget 'should's and ought's'. In our experience the group is there to help each other in personal exploration, perhaps from a different point of view or an altered angle and it is important that encouragement is negotiated, not judgement.

We have found that only basic astrological knowledge is needed to take part, we have had successful insights brought about by people who have only just begun their astrological studies. If anyone taking part is not sure of the astrological symbolism there are always astrologers present to give guidelines on basic ideas and keywords from which to make a starting-point; from this basic premise instinct often takes over. In fact, for these newcomers to astrology, it is less likely that their insight is subconsciously directing their action from a basis of 'knowing' how that planet should be manifesting its energies, therefore the non-logical side can invariably take the lead. The group is often surprised by how active and correct these impressions can be. By letting things take place in this manner those involved are allowing astrology the freedom to become alive and exciting.

Through personal experience we have found and developed certain guidelines that we feel work well. Initially we had no set introductory exercises and we found that going straight into working with a particular chart was often stilted and slow to start off with. We now have various 'warm-up' exercises that we begin the workshops with. These we have discovered help a sense of togetherness to develop. One way of beginning is to attempt to emphasise the fact that each person within the room should be of equal importance, so we decided upon an exercise that would clarify exactly that. For this exercise we ask the participants to go and stand in what they consider to be the most important part of the room. This may be the biggest chair, the centre of the room or even just walking through the door. We then ask each person just to revel for a while in their own importance. They are then asked to state why they feel that particular place to be the most important to them and how they felt about being there. During one workshop where we began with this exercise one particular person felt the fact of just entering a room was the most important. This person chose to stand on the threshold as it meant 'I have arrived, here I am and my arrival is significant to the group.' Yet another person stayed exactly where he was. When asked why, he answered, 'The place where I am is the most important.' By doing this exercise we have had, as you can guess, various responses and reasons, but nevertheless each person finds it significant in his or her own particular way. It aids each participant to accept that although each person's place is different, we should accept that difference as being of relevance to each individual. This is also a good starting-point towards group acceptance and participation.

Another good warm-up/introductory exercise, which we have found encourages people to communicate, is that of asking each person to let their Mercury introduce them and say a few words as to why they have decided to come to this type of workshop. For instance Glenda might say, 'Hallo, I'm Mercury and in Glenda's chart I am in Gemini so I get lots of exercise because she never stops talking. Glenda is hoping to share her ideas with you and also hoping to learn how astrology works for you personally. I could say a lot more but I had better shut up now and let someone else have a go.' Alternatively Tina's Mercury in Scorpio may start of with something like this: 'I hope by the end of the day we have shared many great insights together and developed a much deeper understanding of astrological principles.'

By the end of these warm-up exercises most of the participants are beginning to feel more at ease with each other, as well as beginning to open up their inner channels of listening and perceiving. This is important as our aims are to bring people together in a trusting environment where they can feel accepted and be ready to explore chart factors in greater depth both for themselves and the other group participants. From these beginnings we then follow on to spend the major part of the day working with individuals' charts. At this stage of the day we have no set formula; for instance we do not state that 'today we will look at T-squares, or transits or stelliums'. Instead a natural theme seems to develop during the course of the workshop completely of its own accord. Once the group feel at ease they are asked if anyone would like to work on anything in particular with regard to their charts or current experiences.

It may be that a participant has an aspect in their chart that they find difficult to understand, for instance Mercury in Scorpio, squaring Mars in Leo. If this aspect was chosen to be explored within the group, the person whose chart it is would perhaps opt to act and speak as Mars, asking someone else to act and speak as Mercury. This particular aspect could lead to difficulty in self-expression and this may become apparent as the actors proceed with their dialogue. To experience this as an actor can help a person to recognise certain blockages within themselves and having gained this recognition help them to arrive at a better understanding, perhaps seeing this aspect more as a challenge rather than a continual struggle. In fact just by being involved in the day and working in this inventive fashion can help them to express themselves in a more natural and responsive manner, thus encouraging confidence in communicating their own level of awareness. Creative Astrology helps us to begin to trust in the strength of our own feelings, which can then be used to help someone to clarify a current situation or perhaps understand and change habitual responses that are no longer appropriate in their lives. It can also help one to reach a deeper understanding of how that aspect works for them internally and as such can give a much more objective way of seeing and dealing with their inner motivations.

In every case the natal chart will be displayed for the whole group to see, with the positions of transiting planets also noted. Thus the observers and participants can see what other dynamic may be operating within the chart that can affect the way the aspect manifests. Usually the play starts off by working with the natal chart alone. However, it may be an advantage to allow actors to come in as transiting planets, as this often gives the scene a whole new dimension and can often change the proceedings in a highly dramatic manner. With the chart displayed in this way, if using our example of Mercury square Mars, an observer may notice that Jupiter is currently trining Mercury and semi-sextiling Mars. Intuitively that observer may choose a particular point to involve him or herself in the action to see how this may help with an understanding of the situation. When Jupiter enters the scene at the appropriate point it may encourage both Mercury and Mars to view their situation in a different and more positive way. Jupiter may suggest opportunities and ideas that they may not previously have thought of and this may well be the contributing factor in encouraging faith and giving direction to any areas that may have remained unfulfilled. From the complete interplay of actors and observers the participant who offered the example to begin with can gain a personal understanding of how the aspect can work for them, while the others in the group can begin to understand how the aspect works in a general way. These fresh insights and understandings can often help in other areas of astrological work, as can the basic ideas behind Creative Astrology. Next time you are working on a client's chart, if you come across an aspect and are not sure how it might manifest, try role-playing the planets involved. By taking each planet in turn and speaking as it would speak and even developing a whole conversation within yourself, you can gain surprising insights into the aspect.

Sometimes the participant may prefer to observe the inter-play of planets from a distance. For instance; someone with three planets in Capricorn may ask three others to act out the planets concerned and perhaps a fourth to play the role of Capricorn. The person with this particular configuration can then simply observe the action, and in so doing begin to understand how the planets and sign interact together, and perhaps, how they can be used positively. One such person, observing her chart in action, watched the initial outcome and then asked the actors to play the role from a completely different viewpoint. This turned out to be the very thing that allowed her to see a different approach to the planetary symbolism her chart represented. We have noticed that observers of their own charts find this a powerful way of objectively seeing how planetary symbolism works on a personal level, and how it may be used in positive and alternative ways.

We have explored many facets of astrology by letting the day's theme unfold by itself. On one occasion the theme became Ascendants. It began with a participant who did not know whether she had Gemini or Cancer rising. She asked the group to help her explore the two options. Choosing two people to play the roles of Gemini rising and Cancer rising, she asked them to decide between them who should be on the Ascendant. Joining with the rest of the group she sat and watched the resulting interaction. Both Gemini and Cancer each put their reasons for being on the Ascendant. From the start Gemini was in no doubt that it belonged on the Ascendant and nothing Cancer could say would change Gemini's mind. Cancer tried a gentle approach, became emotional, then moody and finally retreated. During this time Gemini kept up its original assertiveness about being on the Ascendant and indeed appeared to be far more comfortable there than Cancer did. Afterwards the original participant said she felt happier with Gemini's point of view than she did with Cancer's. The group as a whole, having seen the action, agreed. For the participant it was as if a longstanding question had finally been answered. She could of course have rectified her chart or asked another astrologer to do this for her, but this was a far more personal way of experiencing her Ascendant

179

and was therefore more real than any list of figures and dates. Two other members went on to explore their Ascendants in the same manner, but with a third person who had either Libra or Virgo rising, depending on which of his parents' memories was correct, no firm conclusion was reached from the exercise. We opted for the decision that he must have been born exactly on the cusp . . . or could it just have been the uncertainty and indecisiveness of Libra showing itself?

From this point we then went on to explore the charts of people who had difficult aspects to the Ascendant. One person, for instance, had a Gemini Sun that was square her Pisces Ascendant. Needless to say, the Gemini side of things was not at all happy with the Ascendant. This showed when the Gemini actor proclaimed the Pisces to be too 'wishy washy' and emotional to have any effect in her life. Meanwhile the Pisces actor gently held his ground by saying 'I'm here and I'm a part of you, whether you realise it or not.' As the play unfolded, it became clear through this gentle insistence of Pisces, that it played a far greater role in the woman's life than Gemini had previously realised. It was noticed that Pisces brought a shade of gentleness to the Gemini Sun. It was also discovered that Pisces inspiration and dreams were very much a part of her inner life. The Gemini actor at last came to realise this and acknowledge it. Thanking Pisces for its quiet insistence in being a part of her life, the play ended. The woman concerned felt she had discovered something of value about her Pisces Ascendant and from this she resolved to appreciate and consciously use this side of her nature far more in the future.

If there are enough people in the group, sometimes a whole chart will come alive. In one instance this is exactly what happened during the course of one of our workshops. That this happened completely of its own accord, without any prior planning, is a part of the joy of working with astrological concepts in an inspired manner. The person whose chart it was stood in the centre, representing his Sun, while all the other people who were present, acted out a planet each. As the Sun stood in the centre, the planets circled around him busily carrying out their various activities. There seemed to be no co-ordination between the Sun and the planets, nor between the planets themselves. Gradually the Sun became aware of this and decided it was time to make a stand and give the various planets work to do that he felt was relevant to their natal positions. By doing this the whole chart began to work as a team, the Sun then began to plan future progress concerning possible options that were open to him in life. It was a wonderful experience to see this at work, we felt that it gave this person the potential to see how he could take charge of his own life, simply by allowing his Sun/centre to be the guiding factor.

Sometimes during the course of action people can begin to get in touch with a feeling aspect of themselves that has previously remained hidden or buried. By exploring these themes within a caring, accepting group, an individual can begin to develop them further, thus allowing those feelings to be expressed more fully in other areas of life. In this manner acceptance felt within the group environment can begin to encourage the self-confidence needed to express such factors in the outside world. However, it occasionally happens that ways of moving onwards from the situation uncovered are not discovered. At times it seems that having brought the feeling to the light of day it needs to be explored personally by that person before the group can go further. Therefore we never push for a conclusion in this instance and sometimes the participants themselves call the action to a halt. This is a very important consideration as whoever has volunteered their chart to be looked at, in whatever capacity, is *always* in charge. We are not in the habit, nor do we intend to be, of stripping people of their defences, or exposing their private feelings if they do not wish to do so. Only as much as a person wants to reveal at any one moment is encouraged. If previously undiscovered feelings are brought to the surface, it may be because the person involved has reached a time in life when it is right to begin examining these emotions. Although it is important to acknowledge such feelings, it is equally important to allow the person privacy in order to explore them further. Should the person feel they need counselling or further consultation there are always members within the group who are experienced as counsellors and astrologers to whom they can turn.

An example that highlights this happened during one workshop when someone's hidden anger about his career was brought to light, there was no resolution as to how this could be released but the man concerned felt relief at objectively seeing this anger surface. He was an observer at the time and could see through the actions of the players that it would not be as bad to admit to or indeed express his anger as he had previously thought. At this point the man thought that he had explored enough within the group environment and felt that he wanted to work on further exploration alone. In another such case one woman asked for her whole chart to be enacted. The results seemed to be chaos and confusion as all the planets talked at once and wanted to do their own thing. No one planet predominated; each seemed to be of equal importance, which added to the confusion. Some clarification was finally brought to the chart when each planet was asked what he or she felt their role to be within the play. Although nothing positive or conclusive seemed to come out of this exercise the woman concerned felt enormous relief. The chaos and confusion was exactly how she felt her life to be at that moment in time. To see it acted out by others she felt less alone than she had, as she now felt that others had shared in this with her and having shared could understand where she was at in her life far more than before.

At the end of each play, some time is spent reflecting on the insights and lessons that have been brought forth. This involves the players, the director and the observers. This enables a far greater focus on what has occurred as each person's subjective view of the events can elicit different insights. It is also very important for the subject whose chart was being enacted, to clarify their feelings in regard to their own particular concept of what the interaction has meant to them from a personal viewpoint. Such discussion ensures that each play has been explored from as many angles as is possible and this is a method of bringing the play to a final conclusion, at least for the time being.

In order to leave the day in a lighter mode it is sometimes a good idea simply to have a bit of fun, as shared laughter is a good note on which to end. This can be anything you choose, either astrological or otherwise. For an astrological fun exercise we once decided we would each mime a planet, sign or aspect, which the rest of the group then attempted to guess. The hilarity that resulted from this left us all with a positive note on which to release any tensions that had occurred throughout the course of the day. Whether the day's events are serious or light-hearted, the group involvement and awareness is often improved upon. It must be stressed that ours are only a few examples and many more can be thought of and worked with according to the individuals concerned. Whatever you learn to create together in your own groups will be exactly right for you; it's just a matter of allowing your own self-expression to become the reality of the moment.

Authors' Biographies

BABS KIRBY is Vice-President of the Faculty of Astrological Studies and the Director of its Counselling Courses, which she initiated and on which she teaches. She also teaches both certificate and diploma level students in the Faculty's London classes, and is a Faculty delegate on the Advisory Panel on Astrological Education. She is the Press Officer and a founding member of the newly formed (1990) Association of Professional Astrologers, has been involved in humanistic psychology since 1972, and has a private psychotherapy practice. She has lectured and run workshops throughout the UK and abroad (Norway, Holland, Greece, Switzerland and America), using humanistic and transpersonal psychology and astrology, and has co-authored a book (with Janey Stubbs), *Interpreting Solar and Lunar Returns, a Psychological Approach* (Element, 1990).

HANS PLANJE has been fascinated by astrology since childhood, even delivering a lecture about the Sun, Moon and stars in primary school. Eventually, discovering all kinds of regularities and cycles in things that happened inside and around him, he also became curious about that aspect of astrology too. After training for social work, in 1976 he began work as a youth worker, and soon started a training in psychodrama. His work involved a lot of role-play and he used psychodrama techniques to gain insight into, and contact with, individual and group processes in youth groups. At that time he began to have more and more ideas about the combination of astrology and psychodrama. After stopping youth work in 1981, he began to give astrology

184

courses. In these courses, he offered exercises and elements of play so that people could experience the information non-rationally and astrology could be made more practical. This was the beginning of Astrodrama, a practical and experiential astrology which combines basic elements of both astrology and psychodrama. Astrodrama has now become an independent form of astrology which Hans practises in lessons, demonstrations, individual therapy sessions, one-day workshops, weekends and workshops of from one to several weeks, an annual astrodrama course and recently in a three-year training for astrodrama therapists. At the centre is always the participant's own birth chart with all his particular energy patterns, archetypal roots and built-in scenarios. Hans' developing interest in medical astrology also allows him to treat symptoms and diseases in individual sessions with the help of astrodrama techniques. Since 1988 he has published the annual Astrological Diary (*Astrologische Agenda* (Enschede, NL, Astrodrama).

TINA WHITEHEAD was born and brought up on the south coast of England, and moved to London in the 1960s to train as a teacher at Trent Park College of Education. There she specialised in the Art of Movement, an educational course based on the movement theories of Rudolf Laban. She obtained her Cert. Ed. in 1969 from the University of London. After teaching in North London schools, she moved into special education working with children with a variety of special needs. After leaving London in the late 1970s, Tina had the opportunity to develop her long interest in astrology, and has been a practising astrologer since 1982. In the same year she started teaching adult courses in astrology, communication skills and movement for Surrey Adult Education. She was a founder member of the Woking Astrology Group and has been active in promoting networking among local astrology groups. She has led workshops on astrology, both with Prudence Jones and with Lynn Bagnall (circle dance teacher), and enjoys combining her two specialisations – movement and astrology – during her workshops. She has been using Creative Astrology techniques since 1985 and advocates learning by experience in all her educational work. A Council member of the Astrological Association of Great Britain, Tina is also editor of the Astrological Association Newsletter.

JOCHEN ENCKE was born in Cologne, West Germany, and originally worked in the prison and probation service in Germany, later co-founding a registered charity to co-ordinate professional and voluntary services. For two years he assisted in a class for terminally ill children in a disabled children's home, and later in a home for children with special learning difficulties. He then studied psychology and sociology for five years, gaining his *Diplom Pädagoge* (MA in Pedagogics), and simultaneously trained in Neo-Reichian psychotherapy and body-oriented work, later completing a three-year full-time training in Biodynamic Psychology and Psychotherapy in London. He also trained for two years at the Centre for Transpersonal (Jungian) Counselling with Ian Gordon-Brown and Barbara Somers, and did some studies in the analytical field. In 1982 he co-founded the Chiron Centre for Holistic Psychotherapy, leaving in 1984 in order to concentrate on combining psychotherapy with astrology. He has been an astrologer since 1979, having trained first in Germany and then with Liz Greene in London, and now lives with his wife Ulrike in London, dividing his time between his private practice with individuals and with men's psychotherapy groups, writing, lecturing and running workshops in the UK and abroad, and being father to his two children.

ULRIKE ENCKE comes from West Germany and has an MA in pedagogics from Frankfurt University. While at school and university she was involved in voluntary work with the unemployed, the young and the elderly, and especially with the disabled. She was also active in environmental work and in Women's Liberation. She worked for two

186

years as a youth worker for Friends of the Earth, and for 1½ years as a supervisor and leader for consciousness-raising groups in an adult education organisation. Whilst still at university, she trained in communication skills, group dynamics and transactional analysis, and later in body-oriented psychotherapy. She came to London in order to do a full-time three-year training in Biodynamic Psychology and Psychotherapy, also taking shorter courses in humanistic therapy (at the Minster Centre), transpersonal counselling (with Ian Gordon-Brown and Barbara Somers), and analytical psychotherapy (R. D. Laing/Meyerson). She began working as an astrologer in 1980, having taught herself and attended Liz Greene's seminars, and has had a full-time private practice as a psychotherapist and astrologer since 1985. She now lives in London with her husband Jochen and two children, works with individual clients, runs psychotherapy and astrology groups in England and Germany, gives lectures on these topics, and is currently writing a book about Astrological Psychotherapy in German.

HELENE HESS lives in West Wales with her family, where she runs her own craft business, although previously she graduated and worked as a psychologist, where her main field of interest was adolescent development. She began studying astrology in 1975, and during her years in London she co-founded the Hermes Astrology Group, which met until the early 1980s. Helene has studied and practised the Western Mystery Tradition for over thirteen years, her main area of focus being the Celtic Mysteries and the Cabbala. She is particularly interested in exploring the practical use of myth and symbolism as a means of self- and spiritual discovery. She teaches on both her areas of interest in Britain and Holland, and as an author has published the *Zodiac Explorer's Handbook* and contributed to *Voices of the Goddess*, edited by Caitlín Matthews.

PRUDENCE JONES began studying astrology in 1977. After training as a humanistic therapist from 1978 to 1981, she

began to apply therapy techniques to the practice of interpreting horoscopes, running many workshops and an ongoing group in Cambridge, London and the Home Counties.
Prudence understands astrology as a primary means of
aligning ourselves with the cycles of the cosmos, of restoring
the partnership between humanity and Nature, and from
1983 to 1984 she gave a weekly political astrology broadcast
on local radio. She now writes a regular column on the
subject for a local magazine. From 1984 to 1989 she was
a prime organiser of the Glastonbury (now Oak Dragon)
Living Astrology Camps, and she is a regular speaker at
the Astrological Association. Her astrological publications
include three pamphlets on ancient calendration, *Eight and
Nine, Sundial and Compass Rose* and *Time and Tide*, (Fenris-
Wolf, 1982, 1990), and research articles on astronomical
techniques in astrology (*History and Astrology: Clio and Urania
Confer*, ed. Annabella Kitson, Unwin Hyman, 1989; and *The
Urania Trust Handbook*, ed. Charles Harvey, 1990). She has
been involved in the Neopagan revival for many years and is
the co-editor (with Caitlín Matthews) of *Voices from the Circle:
the Heritage of Western Paganism* (Aquarian, 1990).

PALDEN JENKINS is a 1950 9th house Virgo, with Sagittarius
rising and Gemini Moon setting. He says he was saved
by Dane Rudhyar's astrology in the 1960s at LSE, after a
psychology degree course failed to answer what he was
trying to find out. His growth path has moved through
psychedelics, Buddhism, therapy, midwifery and magical
work over two decades. He learned astrology by studying
personal transits for years, began teaching and counselling
in Scandinavia in the mid-1970s, and founded the seminal
Glastonbury Astrologers on returning to England in 1980.
In 1983 he started the Glastonbury Gatherings, of which the
second was an astrology gathering, and the first Glastonbury
Living Astrology Camp was held as Pluto entered Scorpio in
1984. The Oak Dragon Camps and family followed in 1987,
and Palden will be extending them to the USA in the 1990s.

He is the author of *Living in Time* (Gateway Books, Bath, 1987), and is currently working on *An Historical Ephemeris BC 600 – AD 2200* and *A New View of History*.

LINDSAY RIVER has studied astrology and interpreted charts since 1973. She set up an astrological practice in London in 1984, and has taught workshops and classes for many years. In 1987 the Women's Press published her book (with co-author Sally Gillespie) *The Knot of Time – Astrology and Female Experience*. She is trained as a homeopath and practised and taught homeopathy from 1984 to 1989. She now works for a voluntary organisation campaigning for health for all and for the rights and needs of health service users. Lindsay retains her interest in and love for homeopathy, and continues a small astrological practice, as well as pursuing her interests in mythology and in ancient cultures which have represented women and goddesses in ways that disrupt the assumptions of patriarchal society. She sees herself as a cultural worker at the interface between the mystical and the political, criticising the enthnocentric and individualistic approach of much 'New Age' thought, but challenging a rigidly materialistic view of reality and concerned that opportunities for self-discovery and healing should be made available to all. She is currently completing a novel for young people set at Wookey Hole in Somerset.

TINA COX has been a student of astrology for the last twelve years and has been actively involved as Secretary in organising the Suffolk Astrological Society since its inception ten years ago. She is very much interested in counselling and uses this as an important part of her astrological work.

GLENDA COLE has been Chairman of the Bury St Edmunds-based Suffolk Astrological Society for nine years. An astrologer of ten years' standing, she currently teaches astrology at the West Suffolk College.

189

Glossary

Abreaction Usu, 'of the affect'. Acting out and discharge of a stored emotion ('affect').

Active imagination Technique of imaginative exploration developed by Jung. Similar to *guided imagery*, often involves role-playing the figures of one's dreams or spontaneous fantasies in order to become familiar with *unconscious* contents.

Affect Psychoanalytical term for feeling or emotion.

Analytic therapy Psychotherapy, usually long-term, based on the work of Freud. It has the aim of uncovering and reversing supposed trauma from early life. It differs from psychoanalysis in details of technique and in that practitioners do not qualify for membership of the International Psychoanalysts' Association, the governing body for psychoanalysis.

Angles Intersections of the *ecliptic* with the meridian and the horizon. Known as the Ascendant, Descendant, Midheaven (MC) and Lower Midheaven (IC), they divide the horoscope into four.

Archetype (In Neoplatonic philosophy and Jungian psychology.) Concept which lies behind or gives rise to particular objects and situations in practical life. It is symbolised by these, but cannot itself be fully summed up in a word or a picture.

Armillary sphere A three-dimensional model of the celestial globe made of concentric hoops representing the Equator, Ecliptic, Tropics, Colures and Polar circles, set within a horizon. It shows the co-ordinates of local space as seen from earth.

Aspects Angular relationships between planets, measured as angles subtended by their radii to the earth as centre. The major ones are conjunction (0°), opposition (180°), square (90°), and trine (120°).

Bootes In Greek mythology, a son of *Demeter*, he invented the ox-drawn plough, and was the first to cultivate the soil. Demeter placed him among the stars as the constellation which bears his name.

Cabbala Variously spelt 'Kabbalah', 'Qabala', 'QBL' etc., means literally 'to receive'. A Jewish mystical tradition, extensively developed within that community under the Roman Empire, and again by both Jews and Gentiles in Europe in the eleventh to sixteenth centuries. Since the nineteenth century, its classification of the universe has become the basis for most ceremonial magic in the West.

Centaurs In Greek myth, a race of wild beings, half human and half horse, who roamed the slopes of Mount Pelion in Thessaly. The most famous of them was Chiron who, in contradistinction to his fellows, was wise and just. The son of Kronos and of the ocean nymph Philyra, conceived while they were both disguised as horses, he was taught medicine, music, prophecy, hunting and other arts by Apollo and Artemis, and in his turn instructed many of the future Greek heroes. Being accidentally wounded by a poisoned arrow from his friend, *Herakles*, he chose to renounce his immortality and was then placed among the stars as the constellation Sagittarius, the Archer.

Chiron Planetoid discovered in 1977 in an eccentric orbit between the paths of Saturn and Uranus. It has a cycle of fifty-one years. Its presence in a horoscope seems to correlate with unexpected resolution and with healing. Named after the most famous of the *centaurs*.

Christian Hero of *The Pilgrim's Progress*, by John Bunyan. He undergoes many perils and adventures in order to reach the Celestial City.

Collective unconscious In Jungian therapy, *unconscious* contents which do not stem from an individual's personal history but are common to humanity as a whole, for example, the expectation of a father or other authority figure. Sometimes used for the unconscious mind-set of humanity or of a community at a particular time, for example, 'the collective unconscious was brewing up a war'.

Countertransference A therapist's inappropriate reaction to a client in accordance with the archaic and inappropriate model *projected* on them by the latter. For example, client had weak mother or father; therapist begins to find difficulty in setting appropriate boundaries for the interaction, and can be manipulated by client.

Demeter Greek goddess of fecundity, queen of the earth and its fertility, mother of *Persephone*, Great Mother of the world and central figure in the Eleusinian Mysteries.

Dumuzi Sumerian god of vegetation and fertility, husband of *Ishtar*, slain by a wild boar and rescued from the Underworld by Ishtar, or in other versions sent down to the Underworld in Ishtar's place after she had returned from her self-initiated journey there. Also called Tammuz.

191

Ecliptic   The path which the Sun appears to follow in its yearly passage through the fixed stars as seen from earth.

Elements   Four states of being, with three signs of the zodiac classified under each, traditionally known as Fire, Earth, Air and Water.

Equinoxes   (Spring and Autumn) Two days in the year, currently March 23rd and September 23rd, when daylight and darkness are of equal length. The Sun's path intersects the celestial equator at these times.

Facilitator   Person in charge of an experiential session whose job is to help participants explore their own growth- or learning-process. This job replaces the more authoritarian roles of therapist and teacher.

Gerda   Heroine of Scandinavian tale *The Snow Queen*, saves hero from having his heart turned to ice by the Snow Queen.

Gestalt therapy   Developed by psychoanalyst Fritz Perls in the late 1940s, it builds upon the Gestalt psychology model of completing an unfinished perception. The client's attention is drawn to: what is (unconsciously) energised but (consciously) unnoticed in the situation – all parts of a situation are potentially relevant, forming part of the figure-ground whole.

Gilgamesh   Hero of Sumerian epic, who in company with his friend and onetime foe, the wild man Enkidu, seeks and slays the fire-breathing forest giant Humbaba. He refuses the love of *Ishtar*, Queen of Heaven, and in revenge she slays Enkidu, after which Gilgamesh goes on a successful quest for the elixir of immortality. The elixir is, however, stolen from him by a serpent, and this results in his eventual death.

Guided imagery   A journey or exploration in the landscape of the imagination, usually led by a *facilitator*, and presented in the form of a waking dream. It is a way for the enquirer to explore the spontaneous images of the *unconscious*.

Heliacal   Lit, 'with the Sun', especially the rising of other *planets* and constellations.

Heracles   Greek demigod, son of Zeus and the Queen of Thebes. Prodigiously strong, famous for the Twelve Labours he peformed in the service of the King of Tiryns.

Holism   Term coined by Jan Smuts in the 1920s to refer to the spontaneous occurrence of aggregates which have a higher degree or organisation than the sum of their parts. Now used for an outlook which respects and relates to everything that is, rather than simply to the 'good' or 'higher' aspects of reality which are

192

pleasant or advantageous to the viewer.

Horary   Type of astrology used to answer specific questions, such as 'Where is my lost dog?'.

Houses   Divisions of local space seen from the viewpoint of the observer, projected onto the *ecliptic* and interpreted as locating the areas of life (such as health, partnership, or legacies) which the signs and planets in them describe.

Humanistic therapy   Psychotherapy which aims at personal authenticity and self-actualisation, rather than at the 'cure' of mental 'illness' which is aimed at in the medical model. Concerned with the unfolding of human potential. Developed from the 1940s onwards, includes well-known schools such as *Gestalt*, *Psychodrama*, Encounter.

Incommensurable   Having no factors in common. Of two or more world-views, referring to one or more classes of objects not held in common, so the entities of one world-view do not correspond in any obvious way to the entities of the other. For example, there is no deity in Hinduism corresponding to the personification of evil which is the Christian and Islamic Satan.

Individuation   (In Jungian psychology.) Realisation of one's innate potential, the reunification of warring elements of the psyche, identification with the greater *Self*.

Introjection   People's tendency to 'swallow' and play out the roles *projected* on them by others.

Invocation   The act of calling down a higher spirit (in religion and magic), or a quality of being (in psychology), to manifest in physical reality.

Ishtar   Sumerian goddess, Queen of Heaven, lady of victory, love and war. She journeyed to the Underworld to visit her sister Ereshkigal, or, in later versions, to rescue her dead husband, *Dumuzi*. During her stay in the Underworld the upper earth became waste; it was restored on her return.

Isis   Great Goddess of the Egyptians, Queen of Heaven, lady of magic and of medicine. She also conferred sovereignty: her name means 'throne', and the living Pharaoh was identified with her son Horus and sometimes depicted sucking at her breast. Her worship in Egypt is traceable back to 3000 BCE, and spread as a major State and popular religion throughout the Hellenistic world after Alexander's conquests in the fourth century BCE.

Latitude, Celestial   Distance of a planet north or south of the *ecliptic*, measured in degrees.

Longitude, Celestial   Distance of a planet east or west of the spring

Equinox point on the *Ecliptic*. Measured in degrees.

Macrocosm   Lit, 'greater order', the universe, especially the world of the *planets* and constellations, contrasted with the *microcosm*, or individual situation.

Maelduin   Irish hero who sailed to the Otherworld in search of his father's murderers. He had many adventures and visited a host of islands, but never returned to the world of mortals.

Mandala   A circular diagram, usually divided into four sectors. An image of wholeness.

Microcosm   Lit, 'lesser order': the individual human being or human situation, contrasted with the *macrocosm* or impersonal universe of the astronomical and astrological cycles.

Mundane   The branch of astrology dealing with social and political trends, the world as a whole.

Natal   The branch of astrology dealing with the horoscope for the birth of an individual or the inception of an event.

Odysseus   Son of Laertes, king of Ithaca, one of the Greek leaders in the Trojan War. Homer's *Odyssey* describes his twenty-year journey home from Troy and his reunification with his wife, who had remained faithful to him throughout.

Orrery   A mechanism designed to represent the movements of the planets around the Sun by means of clockwork. Called after the eighteenth-century Earl of Orrery, who had one made for him.

Osiris   Egyptian god of fertility, identified with the fertile plains of the Nile valley, husband of *Isis*. After being dismembered by his brother and enemy, the desert god Set, he was restored by Isis through her magic, but later became lord of the Underworld and judge of the dead. He was the patron of immortality, every dead Pharaoh was said to have become Osiris, and appropriate funerary rites would enable other mortals to 'become Osiris' and gain eternal life.

Parallel   Of the same celestial *latitude*.

Perestroika   (Russ., lit, 'restructuring') used especially of President Gorbachev's social liberalisation and dismantling of the Soviet political system in the USSR from 1985 onwards. Hence: restructuring for regeneration.

Persephone   Daughter of Zeus and *Demeter*, called 'Kore' (maiden) before Hades abucted her to the Underworld. After eating of a pomegranate in Hades' realms, it was decreed that she should live for part of the year below ground with Hades, and part above with Demeter. Her name means 'destroyed by death' or 'destroyer of death'.

Planets In astrology, the eight planets, Mercury, Venus, Mars, Jupiter, Saturn, Uranus, Neptune and Pluto, plus the two luminaries, Sun and Moon.

Progressions A method of timing the unfolding of a *natal* or other *radical* chart, usually by reading the planetary positions for one day after the date of birth for every year after the year of birth.

Projection People's tendency to misperceive others as embodying their own unconscious inner pattern, 'projected' out as if on a movie screen.

Protagonist Player of the leading or central part in a *Psychodrama* enactment.

Psychodrama A method of accessing the *unconscious* by role-playing a person's inner dialogue or situation, developed by Jakob Moreno in the 1920s.

Psychodynamics The psychological forces at work in any human interaction, often leading people to misperceive others in accordance with their own unexamined presuppositions.

Psychosynthesis Therapeutic approach developed by Roberto Assagioli (1888–1976), which involves not simply analysing the origin of an individual's psychological patterning, but synthesising the various components into a coherent *Self*. Includes a *transpersonal* element.

Radix, Radical The reference horoscope, against which transits, progressions, and so on, are measured. Term often used for a natal horoscope.

Resistance Unconscious reluctance to confront and resolve any given psychological issue. Can take form of, for example, 'forgetting', paralysis/or incomprehension.

Self (with capital 'S') The whole psyche, conscious and *unconscious*, as opposed to the lesser self (small 's') or conscious ego. Sometimes called 'higher', 'deeper' or 'greater' Self.

Solstices Two days in the year (currently 21st June and 21st December) when the Sun appears to be stationary in its path through the *Zodiac*, intersecting the Tropic of Cancer and the Tropic of Capricorn respectively.

Stellium A group of three or more planets within one sign or four or more within 30° across signs.

Subpersonality Used in *psychosynthesis* to refer to a coherently functioning persona within the overall psyche, for example one's 'parent' subpersonality, one's 'employee' subpersonality. Subpersonalities often clash and must be reconciled in conscious awareness; sometimes they are consciously denied but unconsciously energised and so act independently of the conscious self (as in 'I don't know why I behave like that in these situations').

Symbol Image or stereotype which represents an *archetype*. Contrasted with a 'sign', which refers to a particular object or state of mind, for example, trembling hands being a sign of nervousness but perhaps, like a butterfly, being a symbol of the soul. The symbols used for a given archetype vary from time to time and from place to place.

Synchronicity 'An acausal connecting principle' (Jung): meaningful coincidence without any apparent physical or logical cause. Tends to happen at moments of highly charged emotion.

Synergistic A state in which the many components of a whole naturally and spontaneously function together harmoniously, without conscious restraint or deliberate effort.

Synodic year The solar year defined by the *Solstices* and *Equinoxes*.

Temenos (GK: lit. 'place cut off') An enclosure, usually a temple precinct.

Transference In analytic therapy: a person's tendency to react to others inaccurately as though they were living out roles once played by important adults in the subject's childhood.

Transit The movement of a planet, part or angle relative to the *Longitude* of any feature of the *Radix* chart.

Transpersonal psychology The study of group-consciousness, and the spiritual and mystical components of the human psyche which are outside normal ego-awareness.

Unconscious The part of each person's psyche which is unknown to them but active in their life, causing apparently accidental actions and apparent coincidences. Because it is unknown it is experienced by many people as problematic.

Western Mystery Tradition So called by the magicians of the Golden Dawn (f. 1888), in distinction from the oriental system, Theosophy. A synthesis of Cabbalistic magic, Celtic, Egyptian and other god-forms, alchemy, Tarot, astrology, and so on. It has been until recently a product of the Hellenistic Near East, but is now being enriched by modern rediscovery of the North European native tradition.

Zodiac The belt of constellations through which the *ecliptic* runs. Because of the precession of the *Equinoxes*, the signs of the zodiac in Western astrology are no longer identical with the constellations after which they are named, but are 30° sectors of the ecliptic beginning at the Spring Equinox point, conventionally identified as 0° Aries.

Index

INDEX

125, 129, 138, 154, 166, 176, 177
Mesopotamia 149
microcosmic, microcosmically 15, 90, 104, 105
Midheaven/MC 63, 91, 94, 95, 98, 106, 120, 121, 124, 125, 138, 154
mole, visualization concerning 24–34
monodrama 44
Montessori, M. 50
Moon 15, 33, 46, 53, 55, 58, 60, 61, 74, 76, 79, 80, 87, 89, 90, 100, 101, 109, 121, 134, 135, 136, 137, 138, 140, 144, 145, 146, 147, 149, 154, 164
 as Osiris 150
Moreno, J. 39, 45
mundane astrology 1
 astrology of collective, 36–8, 46–7
 political events related to individual events 83

narcissism 73
natal chart 3, 34
 birth chart 9, 47, 63, 68, 142
 horoscope 5, 6, 12, 14, 34, 111, 114, 178
 individual horoscope 83, 84, 177
Neill, A.S. 50
Neptune 27, 39, 41, 55, 58, 74, 75, 76, 77, 79, 101, 103, 104, 111, 136, 137, 144, 152, 170
New Age 2, 36, 38, 86
'Nicole' 74–9, 80–1
non-invasive see invasive

O'Neill, M. 64
Odysseus 150
Orbis School of Creative Astrology 9
Orphiucus 100, 106
Orrery Dance 139
Osiris 150

pagan
 festivals 87, 88
 listed, 88–9
 rites 86
Pan 103
parallel note, 107
Perestroika 147
Persephone 150
person-centred 11, 50–1
 child-centred 49–50
 client-centred 11, 17, 50
 pupil-centred 11
 student-centred 48, 49
'Petra' 74–6
Pisces 54, 88, 111, 113, 125, 129, 137, 145, 146, 153, 180
Planetary Ball 41

planetary walk 41, 46
Pleiades 95, 99
Pluto
 god 100, 101
 planet 30, 41, 61, 64, 74, 76, 80, 116, 117, 136, 137, 138, 146, 147, 152, 154, 163, 165
Pollux 100, 101, 105
Pottenger, M. 8, 16
pow-wow 132–3, 138, 139, 143
 archeo-astronomical 139
precession 92
prediction 1–3, 5, 6
process (method of creative exploration) 133–7
projection 13
Prometheus 101
 Promethean 103
protagonist (in psychodrama) 44, 45
Psyche 2, 7, 9, 32, 34, 35, 71
psychoanalysis 4, 7
psychodrama 35, 39, 43–6, 63, 140, 143, 148, 184
psychodynamics 6, 111, 174
 group dynamics 67, 74, 81, 84, 132, 140
 inner dynamics 74, 76, 80, 84
 intra-personal dynamics 63
 large group dynamics 14
psychological astrology
 origins of 2–5
 redefines psychodynamics 13
psychosynthesis 4, 20
Ptolemy 37, 107
pupil-centred learning see person-centred

religious 2, 5, 82, 86, 92, 118, 123
 religion 87
research, use of Creative Astrology in 9–10, 16, 123–7
resistance 119, 121
right brain 18, 22, 26, 104
rite 86, 141
ritual 11, 15, 38, 39, 85–7, 89–92, 94, 99, 104, 105, 106, 107, 118
 as exploratory technique 46–7
 as technique of planetary enactment 35, 37, 85ff
Robson, V. 95, 108
'Rod' 71–2, 73
Rogers, C. vii, 11, 50
role-play 7, 13, 17
 techniques 173–5
 see also psychodrama
Rousseau, J-J. 50

199